International Corporate Identity 1

International Corporate Identity 1

Editor: Wally Olins

General Editor: Conway Lloyd Morgan

Laurence King

Published 1995 by Laurence King Publishing

A catalogue record for this book is available from the British Library.

ISBN 1 85669 037 7

Designed by Jason Claisse at Imagination, London

Printed in Hong Kong

Contents

Corporate identity and design Wally Olins

The term 'corporate identity' seems to have emerged in the 1950s. Some say it was first used by Walter Margulies, head of the distinguished New York consultancy Lippincott & Margulies. He was anxious to differentiate his company's work in creating complex and coherent design programmes based on detailed investigation and analysis for some of America's largest companies, from what he regarded as the more superficial one-off graphic design work produced by some of his contemporaries and competitors at that time. 'Corporate identity' may have been a term intended, as we would now say, to add value and differentiate the more complex consulting-based project from its design-based peers, but if that was the intention it didn't work. Within a very short time the term corporate identity, no longer in quotation marks, became standard and everyone was using it, regardless of whether their work involved the reorganization and re-presentation of a major multinational company attempting to manage change and create a new idea of itself for all of its audiences, or whether it was a letterhead for a tiny software house. The very confusion Margulies was trying to avoid has in fact been perpetuated by the phrase he devised.

International Corporate Identity demonstrates the nature of this dilemma, one of several facing the corporate identity discipline. Large, full colour illustrations dominate its pages. The text seems to play a secondary role. Most of the work that is shown in the book will inevitably be judged by the reader almost exclusively on the basis of what it looks like. Moreover, *International Corporate Identity* not only looks like a design book but it will be sold as a design book. It will be placed on the shelves of bookshops throughout the world somewhere between 'Architecture' and 'Art'. Few, if any, copies will appear on shelves marked 'Management' or 'Business Studies'. This book, then, may be perceived by some as perpetuating the assumption that corporate identity is a term for the design of a company's notepaper, vehicles and other assorted visual paraphernalia - other books on corporate identity and design management have been misperceived in the same way, after all. The size and complexity of the corporate identity programmes illustrated, the nature of the brief, the positioning of the organization in the marketplace, will have much less significance than the one simple issue 'what does it look like?', in the reader's mind. However, while some corporate identity designers do still see the visual solution as the beginning and end of their brief, many of its practitioners claim that corporate identity is part of a much larger and more complex picture.

The confusion over the meaning of the term itself is reflected in the way the profession works. On the one hand it is clear that one species of corporate identity consultants is moving onwards and upwards into a kind of management consultancy activity. They take the view that by introducing and sustaining a major corporate identity programme an organization can help to clarify and make visible its structure and strategy, and articulate its vision. The organization will do this so as to differentiate itself from the competition, gain market share and underline and emphasize the new direction that it is taking. In my experience, major corporate identity programmes, by which I mean those produced for large organizations, are increasingly falling into this category. In this kind of situation corporate identity embraces a complex network of management disciplines such as organizational behaviour, marketing, communication and research and almost always design in its various relevant forms. Design in this context does not always enjoy the primary or central position, but it is usually the primary means by which the new positioning is presented; it is therefore one of the most significant tools of the corporate identity specialist.

On the other hand, there is another school of corporate identity which remains influential; this is based around the overwhelming primacy of design, especially graphic design, as virtually the sole vehicle of corporate identity. There are many graphic design companies who follow this path; some of them produce work of an extremely high standard. They usually work for organizations who see corporate identity in terms of a symbol or logotype, stationery, vehicle liveries, signs and all the rest. For these design consultants and their clients, design is everything that the job is about. From time to time, when they are faced with a difficult technical problem, say in financial services or transport, such design companies may call in a freelance expert to help them; they may work with writers and (perhaps less willingly) with researchers, but the base from which they do all their work and their thinking remains graphic design. And they regard their success or failure by the brilliance of the design work that they produce.

Both of these schools, and I am deliberately polarizing them for the sake of clarity, are represented in this book. But because of its format *International Corporate Identity* must seem to have a built-in bias in favour of corporate identity programmes in which the visual aspect is the most striking component. This has posed an inescapable problem for me as the editor. With the best will in the world it is difficult to judge entries from the two different schools on the same terms.

In the first case the design work is the end result of what is often a complex, even tortuous process, which may lead to a major repositioning. But more often the change in the design itself may be relatively modest. It may be thought, for example, that it is essential to retain as much of the older identity as possible to preserve existing marketplace equity. Because of this, the design is often evolutionary, certainly it is rarely radical. Relatively minor modulations of an existing symbol or logotype are applied with obsessive thoroughness to every aspect of corporate operations, modified here or there in terms of colour or shape or style to make a marketing, communication or behavioural point. In pure graphic design terms this kind of work is unlikely to be breathtaking although it may be highly competent. In order to judge the effectiveness of such corporate identity programmes as a whole it is essential to look at the design work within the context of the entire programme. This involves looking at what the company is trying to say about itself, where it wants to be in the marketplace, and similar questions. Siegel & Gale's work for National Semi Conductor (illustrated here) must, I think, fairly be placed within this category.

In the second case, what you see is what you get. The design work that is presented is the beginning, middle and end of it. If the design work is brilliant and original, like Pentagram's work for Spaghetti Recordings, for example, then it is quite fair to pronounce the corporate identity (if that is what it is) a success.

In selecting the entries I have tried to sustain a balance between the consultancy-based approach and the design-based approach. The divergence between the two types of work is now so great that it is at least debatable whether both types should be included in the same book. On balance I believe it is correct to do so, because both schools are representative of the current state and best practice in the art of creating corporate identities.

Corporate identity today

All this is, of course, indicative both of the way in which approaches to identity creation have changed and the way in which the scope of the activity has broadened. Today identities are created not only for corporations but for major brands and their retail outlets. Within the public sector, identity programmes have also flourished, not to say proliferated. Which charity, opera company, orchestra, university or hospital can today do without its identity? As new nations and regions pop up across the world, each has its flag, emblems and all the other paraphernalia associated with self-expression. Norway, Portugal and Canada, for example, all have real, recognizable identity programmes.

Times have never been so buoyant, nor so confusing, for those involved in creating and sustaining corporate identities, as the selection of recent work in *International Corporate Identity* demonstrates. How different, and, comparatively speaking, how recent, all this development is. Thirty or so years ago when I first came into this business, there was no recognizable corporate identity activity. There were plenty of small graphic design companies operating on an *ad-hoc* basis, doing exhibition stands or letterheads and even logotypes and symbols either directly for clients or for their advertising agencies. In some businesses, notably airlines and shipping companies, corporate livery or house style was the norm, but for the most part corporate identity in its current sophisticated or even unsophisticated form did not exist.

So how has the change come about? There is, I believe, a complex network of reasons, but they are all based around three main factors. The first is to do with the competitive environment. The best companies today, in whatever field, create very good products. But in order to win in the marketplace that alone is no longer enough. The companies behind the products have to distinguish themselves emotionally - they have to be liked more than their competitors. This is what the idea of 'value added' means. To borrow a political metaphor, they must win the hearts and minds of the public. This is where successful corporate identity comes in. It works not just on products and services but in environments and (a non-design issue, but one corporate identity experts often consult on) in behavioural issues too.

The second factor is also to do with the wide variety of audiences with which identity programmes interface. Until a couple of decades ago most companies only regarded one audience as really important - the consumer. Today any successful company knows that it has to deal with the needs of its employees, its suppliers, the local community, the financial world - a vast network of audiences as well as the customer. Only corporate identity has the reach to encompass all these audiences with modulations of the same message. The identity of the corporation becomes both the glue which binds together its various parts and the signal to the multiplicity of constituencies with whom it deals. Rare among corporate resources, it has both an external and an internal impact.

There is a third factor affecting the growth of corporate identity and this is the growing number of mergers and acquisitions including what are increasingly being called 'virtual companies'; that is to say those organizations formed through the strategic alliance of several companies who come together to work on a major project. Airbus Industrie, formed from French, German, British and Spanish interests is a well-known example of this phenomenon, but there are many others. Their corporate identities, calling for a nice sense of balance between competing and conflicting organizations on the part of the designer, pose new challenges to the corporate identity industry. All this serves to underline and emphasize the fact that corporate identity has now come of age as a significant factor in contemporary society. The corporate identity discipline is mutating constantly; it faces challenges and opportunities from all areas. It has developed into a powerful tool operating within the context of what is frequently but incorrectly called the marketing services world. Since it has to be seen to fit in somewhere, let this position suffice, at least for the time being. The changes which continually take place in the world scene, politically, industrially and culturally, are directly reflected in changes which take place in the identity business. Let me take two specific examples to indicate what I mean. They are the new technology and the concept of nationality versus internationality.

Technology

The technological revolution has affected the world of corporate identity profoundly. Electronics is replacing paper or supplementing it here as elsewhere. This means firstly that cumbersome printed design manuals, huge volumes of frequently self-adulatory material painfully recording the corporate identity programme, are being replaced by more flexible, more accessible and workmanlike pieces of software which are much easier to use and so have much more chance of entering the corporate blood stream. Secondly, that multimedia developments are forcing corporations to capture the screen for the purpose of projecting their own identity. Much of the multimedia work that we currently see may be technologically advanced, but in graphic terms it is still primitive and crude. Although we had virtually no on-screen entries for *International Corporate Identity*, I believe that we shall see an explosion of work in this field shortly. It is also clear to me that both of these developments will give greater opportunities for corporate identity programmes to penetrate corporations and their audiences at all levels.

Nationality and internationality

Would it be possible by looking at the pieces in *International Corporate Identity* to guess from which country each work originates? In a few cases, perhaps. But for the most part, I don't think so. We had entries from over twenty countries. Most of the entries came from Europe, the United States and Japan, but those places are after all where the overwhelming proportion of corporate identities originate. So perhaps what we received represents reasonably the existing situation. The impression that emerges is that the global corporations, wherever they come from, are perhaps understandably anxious to look at home wherever they go, and so they eliminate, so far as they can, their original national characteristics in favour of trying to develop an international corporate style. The risk with such an approach is that the end result will be bland and anonymous. Smaller companies with a more local audience can afford to rely more on quirkiness and even on domestic visual tradition. But this sometimes deteriorates into silly pastiche.

Then there is the influence of the consultancies that create the work. In a number of countries there still remains a powerful and idiosyncratic graphic design tradition. Within Europe, the Dutch, the Germans and the British, for example, all have strong graphic design idioms, each with its individual character. Inevitably, though, as communication becomes easier and more people see the best from everywhere, and as more designers move not just from one company but from one country and one continent to another, identity work becomes more universal and less national in its appeal. And it is sad but true that books like *International Corporate Identity* encourage this new internationalism amongst young designers.

In conclusion

After having looked at over three hundred examples of new work in corporate identity for this book, against a background of having worked myself on much the same number of projects as a corporate identity professional, I think there are three lessons here. Firstly, we have to learn how to judge corporate identity programmes on criteria which include design but take into account a mass of other factors as well. Secondly, we can look forward to developments in technology influencing the corporate identity world in the future. Thirdly, we have to accept the rise of the global idea in corporate identity. And above all, we see and will see the growing importance of corporate identity for corporations and other organizations, including even countries, as a key strategic resource, uniting corporate strategy, communications, marketing and organizational behaviour, just as Walter Margulies believed it should do when he coined the term.

London, 1995

Corporate Identity in Practice

Wolff Olins at work Conway Lloyd Morgan

In his introduction, Wally Olins argues the case for evaluating corporate identities on task-based criteria, in which the purely visual questions are subsumed into wider parameters. In other words, success in the task of achieving objectives should be the main criterion, and this means that judgement should be based on more factors than just appearance, although design must remain an important element. In some cases these two areas of task and design overlap considerably. In the case of a small company, for example, the graphic quality of a new corporate identity should convey all the positional information the company wishes to impart. Take The Workroom's letterhead for a firm of accountants. The careful choice of colours, and the relaxed but formal typography suggests a small firm interested in working with small, modern businesses. (The accountants in fact number several design companies among their clients.) It is difficult to imagine what extra bells and whistles could have been added to such an identity to convey its message more clearly.

The entrance to Wolff Olins'
offices in London.

But with larger corporations there is an
additional level of problems that the corporate
identity design team has to solve. The changes
that trigger the search for a new identity can
come from a wider range of sources - a merger,
a new market orientation, a new corporate
structure - and the targets to whom the identity
has to be delivered include the company's own
employees as much as the company's customers
and competitors, as well as the wider range
of audiences Wally Olins cites in his introduction.
In such cases the corporate identity is often
as much a major vehicle for reorganizing the
internal culture of a company as one for
projecting an external image. Studio Dunbar's
work for the Dutch police force, for example,
was a key part in the amalgamation of what
had been two independent forces, as well as
a vehicle for a new perception of the role and
attitudes of the police.

The case studies that follow in this section show how Wolff Olins, which Wally Olins co-founded thirty years ago, has dealt with a number of contemporary issues in corporate identities in its work. In each case the visual solution was seen as part of the problem-solving mechanism. In fact in the first case, Wolff Olins were asked to consult on the potential use of an existing design symbol.

Portugal

Although Portugal has been a popular tourist destination for many years, and despite being a member of the European Union since 1986, there was a feeling in government circles in Lisbon that the perception of Portugal by its fellow Europeans was at best vague and at worst distorted. The Ministry of Tourism invited Wolff Olins to work alongside them to devise a way of positioning the country, and of heightening awareness of Portugal's qualities. Tourist activity had concentrated on the beaches of the Algarve province, in the south of Portugal. By widening the country's tourist appeal three results were intended: to open more of the whole country to tourism, to extend the tourist season beyond the summer months, and to attract a wider variety of visitors. The government had commissioned a national mascot image from the famous Portuguese artist José de Guimaraes, and they turned to Wolff Olins to help with implementation. The first step, according to Jane Wentworth, team leader for Wolff Olins, was to commission an extensive survey of attitudes towards Portugal in other European countries.

The results of this survey led to the development of a mission statement, positioning Portugal as a country enjoying membership of Europe together with an outward view over the Atlantic, which gave an overall framework to the implementation programme. At the same time an analysis of tourist resources created a double matrix of development potential. One parameter of this matrix was the definition of the potential and amenities of the six regions of mainland Portugal itself, the other a range of activities and facilities (sport, culture and history, wildlife, wine and food, sea and sun, conferences, and so on, plotted on a country-wide basis). Overlaying the two created a series of targets, giving a framework within which the Tourist Ministry could devise specific initiatives, as well as creating subsidiary quality definitions or missions for the individual regions.

These ideas were presented via a major press launch in Lisbon, with a full audio-visual event. They were further refined into a series of leaflets, publications and an advertising campaign, combined with the new mascot, for which the typography was redesigned by Wolff Olins. They also formed the basis for a series of training seminars for tourist office staff. In a reversal of traditional perceptions of corporate identity, the identity for a whole country was thus defined first through words, rather than images. This example stresses the importance of the research phase in developing an identity, for, as Jane Wentworth explains, 'the government knew fairly clearly where they wanted to go, but not how to get there. Our learning curve about Portugal was matched by their learning about the use and application of a corporate identity.'

The mascot by José de Guimaraes in the new identity by Wolff Olins (above) and used as a design element on promotional literature (below).

The main logo.

Orange

If the problem with Portugal was to texture-map an identity on to a country, the question with Hutchison was how to give visible presence to an intangible, even an invisible. Hutchison launched its mobile tele-communications company on to the UK market in 1994.
The British market for portable and mobile phones has grown exponentially since the demonopolization of telephone services in 1984. Since access to the airways is through service providers who offer standard terms, and since a range of handsets can be used for accessing the technology, the Hutchison business had to devise a role for itself as a supplier of service with added value in a crowded market. Such a situation demands that the design work carries the major burden of the positioning. Wolff Olins had earlier looked at a similar challenge, with the launch of First Direct, a telephone-based banking service. Here the problem was to persuade customers that a bank could exist at the end of a phone line, without the reassuring presence of a bank building on the local high street. The fact that First Direct was the first such service in the UK was a great help, according to Douglas Hamilton of Wolff Olins. Another advantage was the choice of name.

Talk. We do it every day. But should we really let the way we communicate rule our lives? From today we take control. No one will be tied down by time or place. And the skies will begin to clear as we enter a wire-free future. Call us on 0800 286 286.

The future's bright. The future's Orange.

Hutchison did not have the same advantage of priority, and Wolff Olins realized that the choice of name could be the key to success. Many of the competing companies used names heavy with technology, and much discussion of the portable phone market was shrouded in technospeak. So the aim was to create a brand name, whose quality, relevance and validity would be immediately evident, and would be emphasized by excellent and consistent graphics, hence the name Orange; so that the end-client would say 'I use Orange', just as one would say 'I drive Ford' or 'I use AppleMac'.

There was some resistance to this approach at first, and part of Wolff Olins' task was to organize a series of seminars and discussion groups to present the new concept to Hutchison telecom's own staff, their managers, engineers and retailers. Creating the right *esprit de corps* was an essential precondition for success in 'getting a rocket-assisted launch for the brand', as Douglas Hamilton puts it. The result has been that the present customer intake rate, and level of billing, is in line with best projections, and that surveys suggest the public have a higher recall of Orange as a tele-communications brand than its competitors. The next phase will be to develop this perception into a deeper awareness of the range of services available.

The 1994 poster campaign (right) drew deliberate parallels with landscape, while the 1995 programme (facing page) uses a calligraphic theme. The new logo (facing page) is the linking factor.

Royal Philharmonic Orchestra

Cultural organizations have always, by their nature, traditionally been visually conscious, investing, for example, in quality architecture for museums, opera houses and theatres. But greater competition for government funding and for commercial sponsorship, and an increasing range of choices for increasingly sophisticated audiences, have led such organizations today to look to corporate identity programmes to improve their position. One of the interesting features of the work submitted for this book was the higher proportion of such work than would have been the case had the selection been made some years ago.

In 1992 the Royal Philharmonic Orchestra, faced with the threat of cuts in subsidies to the London orchestras, invited Wolff Olins to advise them. The solution was to devise a new corporate logo, based on the neck of a traditional violin or cello, and a graphic approach that would unify the Orchestra's different concert series, educational activities, social programmes and recording work. The identity application also makes a point of featuring the support of major sponsors, especially Classic FM. According to Patrick Cox of Wolff Olins, 'the previous logo was seen as too populist, and so we sought an image more in line with the perceptions of target audiences.' In developing a range of posters for the first season of the new logo, a series of natural backgrounds were selected, building a link between classical music and the English landscape. For 1995, attention has been turned to reaching individuals, through carefully designed and planned mailings. These use a set of graphical devices intended to place classical music in the context of parallel cultural activities.

Irish Life

The new logo in printed form (above)
and in relief (top right).

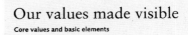

Our values made visible

Core values and basic elements

Irish Life

Define the core activity of the company, and establish a set of values around that core purpose.

Irish Life

Financial services have also seen dramatic growth in recent years, thanks to changes in the structure and regulation of financial markets. One of Wolff Olins' clients is Irish Life. This insurance company had enjoyed a virtual monopoly of the life insurance market in the Republic of Ireland, until competition from the Irish banks and privatization in 1991 made the company aware of its weaknesses. The public perception of Irish Life was of an old-fashioned, bureaucratic institution, and the changes within the organization and outside had left no clear sense of purpose among the staff. Wolff Olins began by researching these questions in more detail, and then ran a series of seminars with a group of top managers to define the core activity of the company, and establish a set of values around that core purpose.

Bryan Boylan, deputy chairman of Wolff Olins, who directed the Irish Life project, is convinced that the consultation process, in which objectives are defined and values determined, is the necessary and central element in working on a corporate identity. 'Sometimes a company will have a clear definition of itself, and all the designer is asked to do is visualize and implement that definition. But in the majority of cases the definition is lacking, or has become distorted or out of date or irrelevant. Restating the core purposes and defining the values of a company is a crucial aspect of management. If the corporate identity expert's work begins and ends with that exercise, it is still a real corporate identity job. It is no longer appropriate to think of corporate identity only or even mainly in terms of graphic and presentational ideas.'

In the case of Irish Life, the core purpose that emerged was 'the whole life'. In other words, Irish Life were not selling a range of different insurance policies, pensions and savings schemes, they were looking after the interests of their clients over their whole lives. Inverting the perspective, from product-led to client-led, focused the purpose of the company. This in turn led to a definition of principles, in which an initial list of over twenty were reduced down, through discussion and consultation, to three - value, leadership, openness.

The visual identity of an abstract human figure emerged from the core 'whole life' purpose: the figure, drawn as deliberately androgynous, stands on a fish, for sustenance, and reaches towards a bird, symbolizing aspiration. The definition of values was in turn the vehicle for communicating the new vision to the employees and then to the clients of Irish Life. Typically, the first corporate identity manual to be produced was not about the use of the new imagery, but a guide to clear and open communications, whether in speaking or on paper, entitled *The Way We Talk*.

The new identity, embodying the new purpose and aim of the company, was launched in 1993, and was accompanied by a reorganization and redirection of the sales force, away from commission agents towards the eventual goal of a staff of advisers able to offer a complete financial planning service. The results of the new initiative were immediate, in that Irish Life rapidly regained market share it had been losing to its competitors.

The presentation of the leadership programme to leading staff members
and the new 'circle of contact' logo on literature about the initiative (facing page)
and on the new baton (facing page, bottom).

Boehringer Ingelheim

Competition and the related issues facing multinational companies are exemplified by the work done by Wolff Olins for Boehringer Ingelheim, a privately-owned pharmaceutical company. Based in the small town of Ingelheim in Germany, famous for its production of red wine, the company has been extremely successful, with, for example, a Fortune 500 listing and operations in over sixty other countries worldwide. Changes in the health-care market, within which the pharmaceutical industry operates, have created new challenges, forcing companies to develop new lines of communication with healthcare providers, whether governmental (as in Germany and Britain) or independent (such as the HMO's in the USA). 'The market revolution is a purchaser revolution, not a consumer one,' John Williamson of Wolff Olins points out. Allocating research budgets strategically has also become a key issue, because of the need to register new drugs for the global, rather than the national market.

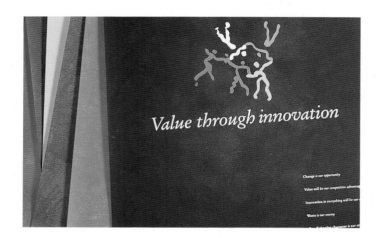

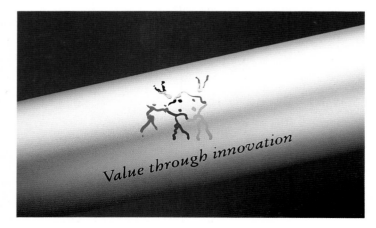

A sample page from the booklet
Our Shared Ambition.

We will only deliver
outstanding value to
our customers if we
are innovative in
everything we do.

The arrival of a new management at Boehringer Ingelheim prompted further consideration of these questions. The company's overseas subsidiaries had traditionally enjoyed considerable autonomy, and were perceived locally as local companies, rather than children of a foreign parent. This had to be preserved while strengthening the links to the centre. What Wolff Olins proposed was a vision and leadership programme. This was developed initially with the board of directors and the directors of the national companies, through discussions, presentations and meetings open to the floor, often chaired by outsiders. (Nick Ross, the British broadcaster, was involved in several of these.) These set out a series of corporate objectives and principles summarized in a simple document entitled *Our Shared Ambition.*

The next task, according to John Williamson, was to present the new message to the company worldwide. The first step was a presentation to selected management and staff at Baden Baden at the beginning of 1994. This was followed by a series of presentations worldwide, made in each case by the board of the company, and by the distribution of training and development packages to the associated companies. While this was a purely internal operation, directed at Boehringer Ingelheim's own staff only, it was treated with the importance and status of a major product launch. This, in Williamson's view, helped reinforce the serious purpose of the message, and the importance the board attached to it.

The initiative is being developed in two ways. The first is a magazine for internal circulation, *Vision*, produced to the highest standards and containing articles that develop and illustrate the central strategy and the worldwide nature of the company. But the content is not restricted to pharmaceuticals - the first issue has an article discussing the problems faced by the European and American motorcycle industry in meeting the challenge of the Japanese, for example. The second initiative is a Vision Day, a yearly event in which the subsidiary companies all round the world would organize events to reinforce the vision and leadership programme. Williamson hopes this will operate as a global wave, beginning in Auckland and following the sun around the world, so reinforcing the common purpose and aspirations of the whole corporation. In tune with this thinking, a baton emblazoned with the new shared ambition logo of a circle of figures, is now used as a merit award. The symbolism is both that of a relay race, and of the Napoleonic baton 'in every soldier's haversack'.

Williamson comments that companies with a strong base in a single country often have difficulty adapting to a wider perspective. Some American companies simply export American practice and attitudes wholesale, expecting their overseas partners to follow. He has real admiration for the way in which the management of Boehringer accepted the challenge of the new programme with commitment and imagination. The Boehringer Ingelheim case is a striking example of a corporate identity project directed primarily at capturing the vision of the staff of a company. It is perhaps a classic case of an internally focused identity.

Forte

At Boehringer Ingelheim the identity process was internally directed. For Trust House Forte Wolff Olins was required to develop an identity against stiff competition, and consolidate the position of an evolved management structure. The identity was primarily externally directed. THF was a second generation company: Charles, later Lord Forte, had built up a considerable empire of hotels and restaurants under a free-wheeling and entrepreneurial management regime. When his son Rocco took over the reins, THF was already a strong institution, but this was now a time for consolidation and restructuring.

The company managed and owned a vast portfolio of names and identities from highly individual luxury hotels to chains of hotels and groups of restaurants, from the Hyde Park Hotel in London and the Plaza Athenée in Paris to the Little Chef group of motorway cafés. 'Their portfolio of names and identities was like a bag of jellybeans', according to Wally Olins, 'in different colours, shapes and tastes.' What was needed was order and shape. The first decision was that the restaurant activities could and should retain their own identities with a minor group endorsement, but that the hotels needed to be linked by a common name to meet the competition of international hoteliers such as Sheraton, Hilton and Hyatt. The name Trust House Forte (the product of an earlier merger) was not appropriate for the hotel trade worldwide, and the acronym THF had little value. So Forte was chosen to link all the hotels and for the group as a whole.

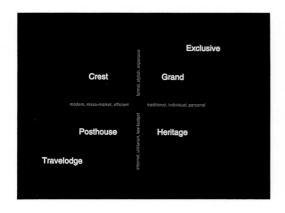

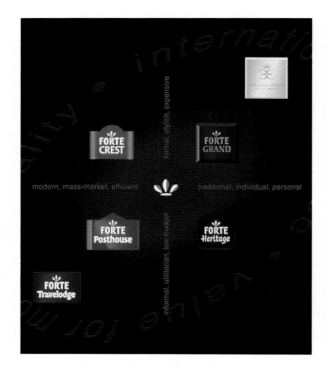

The next task was to classify the hotels by category. Here the simple five to two star rating beloved of guides and tourist boards was too superficial. Instead the hotels were grouped on a grid, 'modern, massmarket, efficient' to 'traditional, individual, personal' along the x-axis, 'informal, utilitarian, low-budget' to 'formal, stylish, expensive' on the y-axis. This grid led to a series of categories - Exclusive, Grand, Heritage to the right, and Crest, Posthouse and Travelodge (existing chain names) to the left. The existing chains retained their brand names, with the Forte title superimposed; the more individual hotels formed collections, in which each hotel retained its own name with the Forte title beneath. This process 'makes heterogeneity a virtue not an encumbrance'. The identity creates choice and diversity, linking Forte with a wide range of hotels grouped into brands and collections, within which established names and reputations such as The Ritz in Madrid or The Bear at Woodstock in England can be sustained.

The carefully developed identity took on the major international competition and successfully improved Forte's market share.

From the management viewpoint, the new classification gave Forte a pattern for future investment, and for staff development. The three years development work, starting in 1991, and the continuing implementation of the identity, shows how a mature programme can be achieved.

Marketing people 6 inclined to c identity as a tool for Marketing 'The corporate brand'

maintaining clear lines of communication with staff, clients, shareholders, and bankers, press

Conclusion

The issues handled by Wo ns with this handful of cases from t   rrent and recent
work are reflected in many of the projects found later in this book. Companies need
to be increasingly responsive to changes in the marketplace, while maintaining clear lines
of communication with staff, clients, shareholders and bankers, press and government.
A well-planned corporate identity programme is one of the keys to achieving this, and is
being increasingly seen as an essential part of the modern corporation's strategic arsenal.
The development of a programme needs careful, often extensive research and planning as
much as it needs graphic imagination. The implementation of a programme requires careful
initial presentation and discipline in a wide range of management resources because
corporate identity affects all aspects of a company's business.

But some senior and middle managers find this overarching power of the identity discipline
difficult, used as they are to dedicated resources in their own sectors. Marketing people are
inclined to see identity as a tool for marketing 'the corporate brand', personnel managers
as 'a weapon for staff development', and so on. But the Zeitgeist is moving towards more
integrated corporate activities, and this means that the range of specialist skills the identity
consultant will have to use will also spread, from multimedia technicians to industrial
psychologists. This wider range of identity activity will sustain large consultancies while also
creating opportunities for small, specialized, even individual operators. New technologies
will also have an impact, as companies, especially in the service area, increasingly turn to
multimedia as a means of communication. This means that clients will inevitably perceive
the company they deal with increasingly through graphics. 'Graphic design will remain
significant in identity' says Olins. And corporate identity will continue to be a growth
business. 'I think the term identity still has strong meaning, but as identity usage spreads
from corporate bodies through the public sector on into national and regional entities,
the adjective "corporate" inevitably becomes less meaningful.'

But as the public becomes increasingly visually sophisticated, as witness the increasing protest
about the visual homogenization of the High Street, so designers will be led to develop
considerable variations within an overall identity programme. As Olins puts it 'In the early
stages of identity - by which I mean up until today - the theme was to repeat a single idea.
This homogeneity will be replaced by variety within a coherent structure. This can only
create greater and better opportunities for creative design.'

La Vourdiat, 1995

International Corporate Identity

New Corporations The Government Corporate

When Robert Blaich was appointed head of the design group at Philips, the giant Dutch electronics company, he was asked at his first board meeting 'what is the cost of design?' His reply was typically robust: 'what', he said, 'is the price of no design at all?' He was highlighting a dilemma many other companies have had to face: the risk of losing market share, public perception and even profits as against the necessary investment in design, not only in product and communications design, but corporate design as well.

The last decade has seen a series of seachanges in the very nature of corporations. Mergers, acquisitions and takeovers, together with more efficient and dispersed corporate structures, and an increasing international field of operations for even small and medium companies, have become the normal pattern rather than the exception. These changes have affected all aspects of a corporation's business and practices, through financial management, production, marketing to, of course, design.

At the same time there has been a growing awareness in the corporate sector of the importance of design as a central element in corporate planning and organization. This process began with companies in the field of consumer products, notably Sony, Canon, Olivetti and Philips, but has been extended through their example, and the advocacy of corporate leaders and design experts, to a whole range of companies in different and wider fields. Corporate identity is no longer seen, in these aware companies, as a matter of logo and letterhead, but a key component in corporate culture, affecting the corporation's relations with its clients and customers, its own staff, its professional advisers, bankers and shareholders, with politicians and civil servants, with the press and in fine with the public at large.

The tasks facing design managers, designers and design consultants have become increasingly complex at the same time. A merger or takeover does not merely put the assets of two companies - possibly previous business rivals - together, it requires the fusion of their corporate structures and attitudes into a new whole. The creation of a new business also demands its careful insertion into what may be a crowded marketplace. The extension of a company's business into new markets internationally calls for a public face that will be recognized across differences of language and social and political cultures.

In the case of a corporation with an established corporate identity, adapting this to new challenges and circumstances must be a delicate and slow process, as radical change can undo as much existing goodwill as it creates new. The proper application of corporate identity is like calving an iceberg: the visible part, on letterheads, vehicles, buildings and publications, is only a small part of the process, which involves presenting the new concept and its related practices to staff and to key investors and customers. After the launch, the progress of implementation of the identity needs to be carefully monitored, to ensure that the values enshrined in the new identity are being communicated properly both within and without the company.

A further impetus to the development of corporate identity has been the increase in privatization or deregulation of activities formerly controlled by central governments, and the appreciation that these need to operate as effectively as their private counterparts. A survey of corporate identity design ten years ago would have included a preponderance of major manufacturing, oil, aviation and vehicle companies dominating the choice. In this contemporary selection governmental agencies, police forces, transport authorities and universities make up nearly half the selection, for they are all aware of the value of quality corporate identity in embarking on their new roles. This first section looks at how these two categories of 'the new corporation' are meeting the question of corporate identity.

Take the section on transport companies: two of these, Air Canada and Cathay Pacific, are traditional independent airlines, who see the regular upgrading of their corporate identity and fleet livery as simply best business practice in an ever more competitive market. But for the Ferrovie dello Stato, the Italian state railways, a major change was in progress, from a government agency to a publicly-owned corporation, and the corporate identity programme is being used as a vehicle for the changes in attitude and practices such a major renewal of corporate culture involves. Finally there is Eurostar, the train linking London, Paris and Brussels using the Channel Tunnel. This joint venture between the French, Belgian and British railways (two state-owned, the other now a series of state-owned corporations, prior to privatization) required an independent identity that would work across national boundaries.

As graphic design solutions each has its own merits, and sets standards for future transport concepts. But the interesting aspect of each design - and this is true for all the designs in this section - is not the graphic solution alone, but how the corporate design programme has been tailored to meet the needs of the company concerned.

• **Politie**
The Netherlands

**New corporate identity for the
merged Dutch police force**

1993

• Joost Roozekrans

Studio Dunbar
The Hague, The Netherlands

The decision by the Dutch Government to merge the country's two police forces, the Rikspolitie, or general police force, and the Gemeentepolitie, responsible for cities and urban areas, led to a competition for a new unified design, won by Studio Dunbar (who had also created identities for the Dutch Post Office and the Dutch national railways).

The brief was not only to create a new identity for the unified force, but also to present the police to the public as a modern, committed and efficient organization, and in particular to distinguish the police force from the private security forces operating in the Netherlands. While the brief was short on the first part, the complexities of modern policing made arriving at a solution far from easy. The problem facing many police forces, not just in the Netherlands, is the balance between the public looking to the police for reassurance and security and the police needing to establish their position where wrong-doing is involved. This is a conflict between authority, which inspires mistrust, and openness, which leads to trust. As Gert Dunbar, founder of Studio Dunbar, puts it, 'There must be a good level of authority in the identity. But the problem is that this is a new sort of identity. The old sort was the easy authority, the hateable kind. But this is new.'

The solution was derived in part from the secondary requirement in the brief. Although the two earlier police forces both used a badge based upon an eight-pointed star (it is a common image for police forces), so did many private firms. Dropping the star, and retaining the grenade and constitution book from the earlier badges, both distanced the new force from the private ones and retained links with the past. The word Politie was also chosen, because security firms are barred from using it, and because, unlike a purely visual symbol, it is a virtual homophone for the word for police in most European languages, and so would be understood by tourists and visitors to the Netherlands.

Dropping the star was, for Dunbar, also part of creating what he terms a 'civilian heraldry', free of military and authoritarian overtones. As part of the same policy, and despite some resistance from certain sections of the police force, name badges also became an integral part of the new uniform. Name badges had been the practice of some of the regional forces, and the decision to include them on all uniforms shows how the new identity played a key role in the complete renewal of the reorganized force - the previous system had up to fourteen different ranks, for example, which are now streamlined into eight. The difficulties of the problem are exemplified by the designer's suggestion that the standard uniform jacket would carry the word Politie in a band 30 centimetres wide across the back. This would, he argued, enable

The new logo (above left) and new exterior signs (above).

officers to be visible, and so accessible, in the street. The counter-argument was that this would expose the police to risk, and in the end this view prevailed. This shows how complex the redefinition of the police's role and authority has been, and how a sensitive and pro-active design policy can play a valuable part.

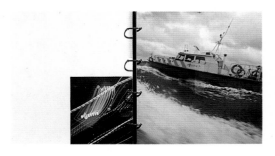

The new uniform (below) includes the logo and name badges.

The new identity applied to vehicles (this page and facing).

• Stirling District Council
Stirling, Scotland

**New corporate identity for a
municipal council**

1993

• Andrew Hunter, Alan Ainsley

McIlroy Coates Ltd.
Edinburgh, Scotland

Changes in the structure and responsibilities of local government in the
United Kingdom have created communication problems for local authorities.
The traditional town and county coats of arms may no longer reflect the
geographical reach of the authority, let alone its position in the hierarchy
of government or its aspirations. So a new class of municipal identities has
come into being, to meet the changed role and changed locations of local
government, reflecting their role as providers of a wide range of services
rather than as a single unit.

The new identity for Stirling District Council in Scotland needed to reflect
the range of services provided by the council, including housing, social
services, leisure, library and sports facilities, refuse collection, financial and
property services, public transport and infrastructure. While the previous
identity had focused on connections with Scottish history and local heavy
industry, linked by a fanciful rainbow, the new identity had to be appropriate
to a mixed economy in which services were replacing industry. The council's
own staff and officers also needed an identity that would provide a central
theme and a set of aspirations in their own work.

McIlroy Coates' solution was a radical one: out went Robert the Bruce and
the Stirling bomber - provoking considerable comment from traditionalists -
and in their place came five stylized figures, composed from a series of
elements that can be linked visually to different aspects of the council's
work - brick walls, spades, football pitches, trees and roads, for example.
At the same time the discipline of two basic colours, a blue and a red,
and a standard logo for the council's name, was also introduced. The family
of five figures, with their no-nonsense, almost cartoon style, provoked
some uncertainty, even shock, at first. According to Paul Crake, marketing
and communications manager for the council, 'the approach focuses on
what it is our customers want us to do.' This is taking place at a time of
'revolution in the way local government works', Crake adds.

The designs were not only a radical departure from the usual solemnities
of municipal imagery, they were also applied in a new way. The five figures
are not allocated exclusively to individual departments, but used by all in
a deliberately-managed random fashion. The 'sports' figure may appear on
a housing van, the 'financial' figure on the libraries letterhead - and the next
sheet of letterhead will carry a different figure. Because the outline of each
figure is generally consistent with the others, and strict rules cover the
placing of the typematter and logo, the result, even in signage, is not
confusing.

Rationalizing stationery production meant that the change was not too
expensive. Further cost savings have been made with vehicles, which are
in white (a standard supply colour) with a blue band at the lower level
and one each of the figures applied to available panels on each side of
the vehicle in red and blue. The identity also functions as a safety device,
following a proposal from Andrew Hunter, managing director of McIlroy
Coates. Many of the vehicles are slow-moving (refuse lorries, street cleaning
vehicles, tractors etc.). They should, he suggested, be emblazoned with
magnified sections of the key identity figures at the rear as a warning to
motorists. The result has been most effective, and is part of the invisible
savings created by the new identity, to be added to the actual savings that
can be demonstrated in its first year in use.

In purely graphic terms, the new identity is a consistent and even witty
piece of work. It is well thought-out, with clear guidelines for application
and use. But its success lies not only in its charm but in the way it
effectively represents a new vision of the council's role. No longer is
the council an abstract authority, but a provider of services. This change
is not only in terms of the council's relations with its users, but also,
and very importantly, with its own staff, whose attitudes needed to evolve
in line with the council's changing role.

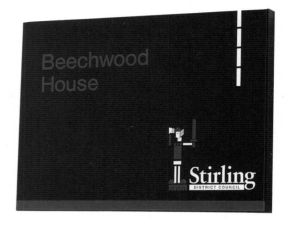

The new logo on signage and letterheads (facing).

St Ninians Local Office
Stirling District Council
37 Modans Road St Ninians Stirling FK7 9BS

Phone 0786 451 066 Fax 0786 451 524

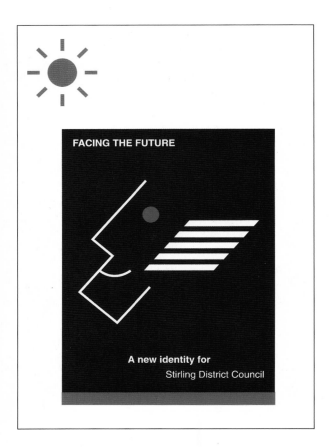

The identity applied to municipal publications.

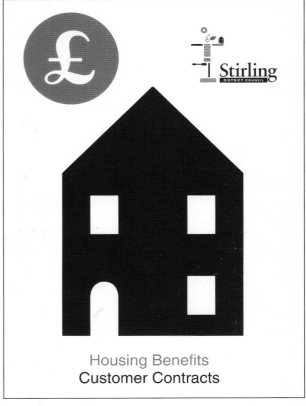

Housing Benefits
Customer Contracts

• **Kadaster**
Apeldoorn, The Netherlands

Corporate identity for the
national land registry

1994

• Ronald van Lit, Constance Kokkeel,
Paul van der Zijden

Tel Design
The Hague, The Netherlands

The Dutch government has a continuing policy of moving government institutions from public ownership to independent status. Such a change of status is not only political and economic, but often accompanies a rethinking of the institution's internal structure and approach to its public. In such a situation a new name and identity serves a valuable purpose in managing the change.

In the case of the public land registry the name chosen was Kadaster, previously the title of part of the service, and one reflecting the original task of measuring and mapping land. The central item in the design is the capital letter K, in a sloped and truncated serif, chosen to echo the shape of the tripods for theodolites used in land surveying. The two main colours are earthy green and yellow, used in solids and tints. They appear on stationery, vehicles, badges and signs, as well as on Kadaster's own publications.

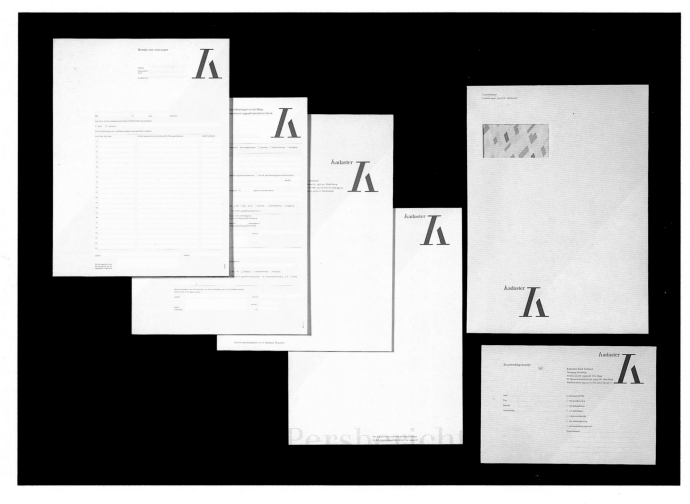

Names badges (above) and publications (below).

Outdoor and indoor signage (left and above),
information packs (below) and vehicle liveries (facing page).

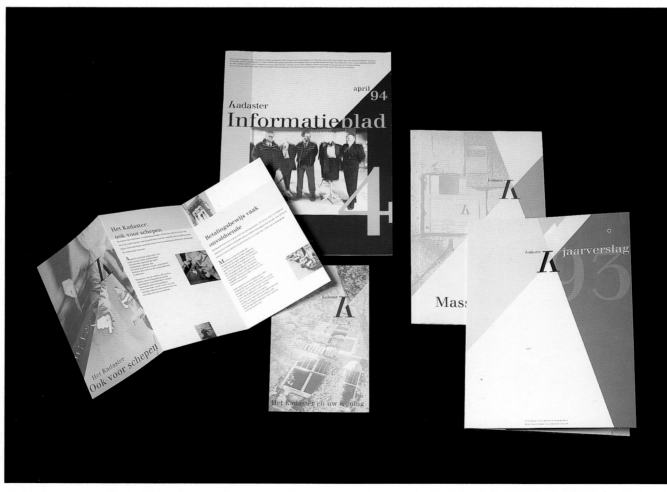

Kadaster
algemeen medewerker Financieel-Economische en Bedrijfskundige Zaken (v/m)
Kadaster
Informatieblad
juni 94
5
Kadaster
Verzelfstandigd! En nu...
Feest in Vredenburg
Marketing krijgt vorm
Kwaliteitsverbetering
Lintjesregen
Normeringsklus geklaard
Inspelen op DIS-ontwikkelingen
Meer verantwoordelijkheden voor de
Kadaster
huiscollectie
Suiker
Creamer
Kadaster
Hoofddirectie Apeldoorn
J.H. Jeuring

• **Sparkasse Rhein-Nahe**
Bad Kreuznach, Germany

Identity for the Rhein-Nahe
region, for a regional savings bank

1994

• Alexander Demuth, Reinhild Singer,
Peter Kraus, Thomas Rohrborn,
Thomas Heise

Alexander Demuth GmbH
Frankfurt am Rhein, Germany

The client bank wished to identify itself strongly with the
region it served, by creating a logo for the region to be used
along with the slogan 'Der milde Westen' ('The mild West').
This would help develop the growth of the region as a business
area, promoting local interests as well as the bank's own.
This is an interesting example of an indirect commission
for a corporate identity.

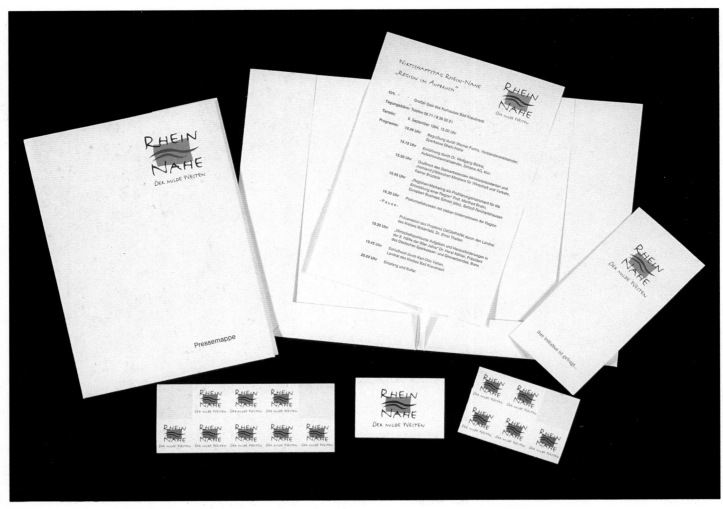

Identity manual

Main logo and slogan.

Promotional advertising for the region.

• **Credis Fund Service AG**
Zurich, Switzerland

New identity for investment
management services

1994

• Zintzmeyer & Lux
Zurich, Switzerland

Credis = Investment Funds

Credis = Equity Funds

Credis = Portfolio Funds

Credis = Money Market Funds

Credis = Bond Funds

Credis = Real Estate Funds

Credis = Funds at work. By Credit Suisse

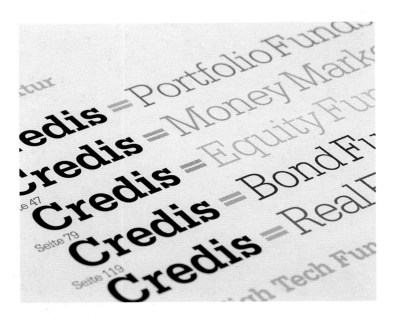

Credit Suisse wished to separate their investment
management services into an independently perceived
brand. The Credis title formed a sufficient link with
the parent, and the new identity is used for print
media, signage and advertising.

• **Postbank**
Amsterdam, Holland

**Corporate identity for the Dutch
post office bank**

1992

• Eugene Bay, Ros Wyers, Peter van
Dewsen, Lilian Vos, Hilde Loohuis

Visser Bay Anders Toscani
Amsterdam, The Netherlands

Although the Dutch Giro Bank had always given the
consumer a central role, changes in the financial
services market both in terms of competition and
towards more open banking led to a redevelopment of
the corporate identity. The light blue colour and the
lion logo were already well established, so these were
strengthened by the addition of a second, darker blue,
redrawn and better-balanced typography and a more
readable lion.

Elements from the redrawn lion logo are used on
promotional material, and as vehicle liveries. This
is part of the process of 'permanently advertising'
the bank to actual and potential customers, while
reinforcing the bank's long-standing policy of directness
and accessibility.

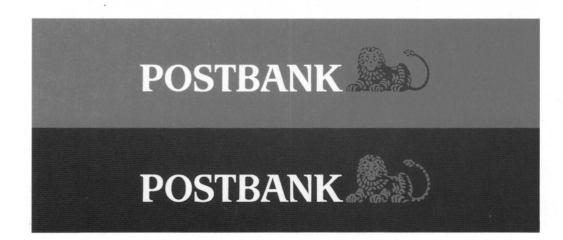

The lion logo as used on literature and vehicle signage.

• **Czech Technology Park
Brno, Czech Republic**

**Logotype, signage and literature
for a new technology park
development**

1994

• Michael Denny, John Bateson, Jonathan Simpson,
Debbie Osborne, Andrew Ross, Rachel Dinnis

Roundel Design Group
London, England

The Czech Technology Park is a joint venture between
the construction company Bovis and the city of Brno,
together with VUT, the city's Technical University.
The Park will provide business, industrial and residential
facilities to a high technical specification. It is intended
for international companies looking for a quality location
in the geographical centre of post-Cold War Europe.
The Park's first phase will open at the end of 1994, and
the final site will cover 120 hectares. Overall architectural
design has been handled by Building Design Partnership.

The logotype C, inset into a concentric ring, emphasizes
this centrality, using the motif of a drop of water falling
and creating ripples. The promotional literature was
developed after research showed the need to communicate
at two levels. The 'Concept' brochure promotes the core
philosophy of the development, using natural images,
scientifically photographed, as visual metaphors and also
to remind the reader that the Park is set in natural
woodland. The 'Development' brochure addresses detailed
questions on the Park, its development and facilities.

The main logo (top) and letterhead (right) with the covers
and a spread from the promotional brochures (facing page).

Central Europe's premier business and technology development

Central Europe's premier business and technology development

concept   development

Czech Technology Park
Brno

Czech Technology Park
Brno

Academic centre of excellence

Established cultural community

City of history and tradition

Brno, a city for 750 years, is at the hub of

historic trade routes which have encouraged a rich

tradition of cultural and business activities.

heritage

It is an established centre of academic excellence

and pioneering research, with six universities which

have influenced many aspects of science, industry and

commerce, ranging from genetics to turbines.

A strong tradition in engineering also exists

from the time when the nation was the world's

seventh industrial power.

University of North London
London, England

Identity for a new university

1993

• Stephen Franks, Judith Johnston

Coley Porter Bell
London, England

The change of status from polytechnic to university offered the North London Polytechnic a window of opportunity to represent itself to the potential student public as the University of North London. Because of its innercity location, the institution had worked hard to care for and support its students, and so it was appropriate that the selection procedure involved staff and students in preparing 'mood boards' with the designers. The key image chosen was of a victorious fencer, arms raised in triumph, and this was translated into the abstract symbol of the new identity, with a colour scheme of deep blue and red to express strength and stature.

● **Caixa Barcelona**
Barcelona, Spain

Identity for a savings bank

1990

● Arcadi Moradell, Josep Vallbona

Arcadi Moradell and Associates
Barcelona, Spain

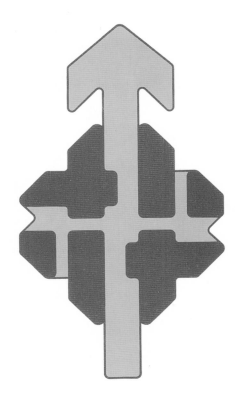

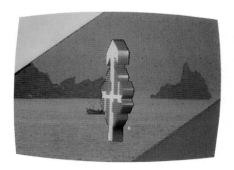

The main logo (above left) uses the traditional Catalan colours of red and yellow, and an arrow as a symbol of aspiration. Its graphic quality makes it suitable for use as an animated item in television commercials (above) as well as in a conventional context, as on a credit card (left).

• **National Semiconductor
Sunnyvale, California, USA**

**Worldmark and Corporate Voice
programme for computer chip
manufacturers**

1994

• Kenneth Cooke, Raul Gutierrez (New York),
Ian Louden (London)

Siegel & Gale, New York and London

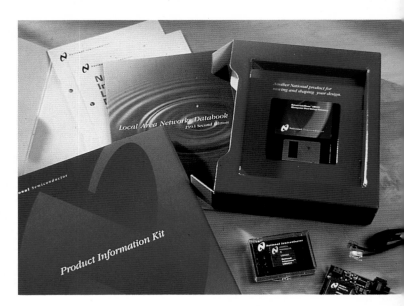

The new logo (top) and literature for the Corporate Voice programme.

The arrival of a new chief executive can often be the catalyst
for change in a corporation. National Semiconductor had been
immensely successful in the computer boom of the 1970s and
1980s, supplying semiconductors and storage devices. But with
the expansion of the computer industry they were increasingly
perceived as suppliers of commodity products rather than
innovators. Gil Amelio's appointment as CEO led to a rethinking
of the company's strategy, placing the company firmly as creators
of technology for moving and shaping information. This
refinement of activity needed to be accompanied by a change
in corporate culture, symbolized by a new identity.

The work was undertaken by Siegel & Gale, with the New York
office providing the main design concept and the London office
the implementation of the new design in Europe. They devised
two elements, the National Semiconductor worldmark, a stylized
letter N, which is for use on letterheads, packaging, products
and vehicles, and the Corporate Voice programme intended
to introduce the new concept to employees, agents and others.
The initial response to these two initiatives has been good,
creating within the company 'a sense of common purpose that
would have been frowned on in the old days', according to
one systems analyst.

• **Renault Vehicules**
Paris, France

Revised identity for a motor
manufacturer

1992

• Identité Visuelle Renault
Paris, France

Motor vehicles badges were among the first corporate identity symbols of the 20th century. Today they are crucial to the market success of any manufacturer's marketing strategy, and represent enormous goodwill and investment. When Renault decided two years ago to redevelop its passenger car identity, (the then existing identity had been created by Wolff Olins in the 1970s) there was no question of dropping the familiar lozenge mark nor the special Egyptian typeface for the name. Rather the lozenge mark was smoothed and streamlined, and the signage, lettering, colour codes and positional relationships redefined.

This 'new' identity also created the opportunity to define very exactly how the various decorative architectural features (flags, masts, entrance frames) were to be used on dealerships and service stations. The need to create a homogenous and so familiar environment for the customer is a key aspect of developed corporate identity practice in a large organization with a high number of outlets. The Renault identity shows how an existing and successful mark can be updated and policed to ensure continuing market success.

The new logo on a vehicle (below), and proposed signage for dealerships (facing and above).

• Harley-Davidson
California, USA

**Corporate identity manual for
a motorcycle company**

1993

• Siegel & Gale
New York, USA

Harley-Davidson is a byword among bikers for their powerful and elegant machines. As with many US and European manufacturers, they came under strong pressure from Japanese competition in the 1970s. Their response was to emphasize the strong tradition of Harley bikes and their place in popular American culture, as well as developing a new and extended range of highly personalized machines, with a wide range of visual and mechanical features. The Harley winged logo was a key element in this, and to promote the company its use was also adopted for merchandise such as clothing.

The success of this policy was considerable, extending Harley-Davidson's market well beyond the USA. But such was their success that preserving their unique identity in a global market became a potential problem: how to communicate the Harley mystique to a new audience of dealers, licencees, communicators and final customers. Siegel and Gale were therefore invited not to redesign the logo, which would have been a disastrous step, but to produce a handbook to the logo that would explain and reinforce the Harley lifestyle and protect the strength of the brand. The photography, typography and design of the book make it a statement of the Harley message in itself. This is an example of identity used solely as a branding mechanism.

INDIVIDUALISM

ADVENTURE

FULFILLMENT

"Harley-Davidson
It is a way to live life to the fullest." (U.S.A.)

*"It starts with the bike,
a vehicle that changes the way you live
your life." (Japan)*

*"You bond closer to the brand, making a
personal statement in the way you dress.
You are an extension of your bike." (Australia)*

*"You share experiences
with like-minded people.
When you're on a Harley, there's an
immediate bond between riders." (Germany)*

The unique and enduring appeal of the Harley® experience. The sight of it. The sound of the motorcycle itself, the core of the Harley® experience. The sight of it. The sound of the Big Twin speaks to basic human emotions on a level so powerful that the Harley-Davidson brand becomes more than a machine. It becomes a passionate commitment to motorcycling as a way of life.

There are three essential elements to the Harley-Davidson experience, which riders feel the first time or the ten-thousandth time they ride: the joy of individualism, the chance to be free, to make choices; the commitment to adventure, the opportunity to change, to discover new experiences and emotions; the reward of fulfillment, an intense, personal and consuming bond with the bike that means a richer, fuller life.

What Harley-Davidson sells is that experience—the most complete and rewarding motorcycle experience. That is our global position. On the following pages are guidelines for consistent marketing communications, from market to market, that will fit the Company's global image.

Einen weltweiten Markt für Harley-Davidson® aufzubauen bedeutet, sich auf die einzigartigen Qualitäten des Motorrads zu konzentrieren, die Faszination des Harley® Lifestyles herauszuarbeiten und die Marke zu stärken. Die Mystik der klassischen und zeitlosen Harley-Davidson Motorräder entwickelt sich aus dem einzigartigen, immerwährenden Appeal. Seine Stärke liegt darin, daß Veränderung nie Selbstzweck ist; elegantes und doch kraftvolles Styling verschmilzt mit Tradition und Innovation. All dies muß das Leitprinzip der weltweiten Harley-Davidson Marketing-kommunikation sein.

Building a global market for Harley-Davidson® means focusing on the unique qualities of the motorcycle, developing the appeal of the Harley® lifestyle and protecting the strength of the brand. The mystique of the classic and timeless Harley-Davidson motorcycle evolves from its unique, enduring appeal. Its great strength is that change is never merely for the sake of change; elegant yet powerful styling melds tradition and innovation. This must also be the guiding principle behind Harley-Davidson global communications.

• The Document Company Xerox
Rochester, NY, USA

• Peter J. Harleman, Margaret Youngblood, Margo
Zucker, David Ray, Paul Travis, Nancy Zeches

Landor Associates
San Francisco, USA

**New corporate identity for
business systems manufacturer**

1994

The Xerox copier is a standard feature in any well-equipped office: the verb 'to xerox' has entered the language as a synonym for photocopying. Few modern products have achieved the level of success of small case letters only! But thirty-five years after the first Xerox machine was launched, photocopiers are only part of Xerox's business. The company wanted a new identity to mark their new position as creators of complete management systems, including storage units, fax machines, scanners and printers. The old name was tied too closely to one particular aspect of their business, and to a view of office procedures that was becoming out of date. The new visual image, a red capital X with a partially digitized ascender, was devised to emphasize the company's technologically innovative role and for consistency with its expanding capabilities. The reversal of the name, which now leads with the words 'The Document Company', is also intended to focus attention on the change of direction. Together the two elements position Xerox at the crossroads of the information age.

• **CSI Corporación Siderúrgica
Madrid, Spain**

**Identity for restructured
steelwork company**

1994

• Alberto Corazón

Investigación Gráfica SA
Madrid, Spain

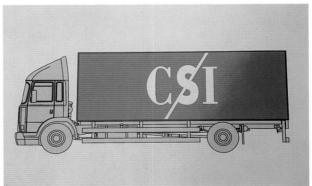

- **Hori Productions Inc.**
  Tokyo, Japan

  Identity for a production company

  1994

- K₂
  Tokyo, Japan

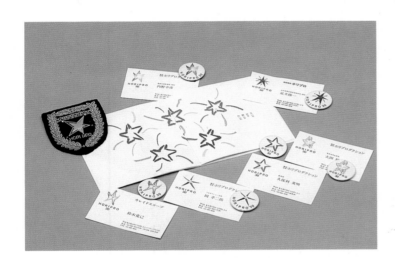

• John Diefenbach, Alberto Levey

Diefenbach Elkins, Alberto Levey & Co
New York, USA,
Buenos Aires, Argentina

• Eg3
Buenos Aires, Argentina

**New identity for a joint petroleum
distribution group**

1994

One of the problems in finding a name for a joint
venture is ensuring that the different partners are
treated equitably, and that the enterprise becomes
a distinct corporate personality - creating synergy
with minimum friction. This was the first part of the
problem faced by Diefenbach Elkins and their South
American partners Alberto Levey when they were
approached by a consortium of three Argentine oil
companies, Isaura, Astra and Puma, who were joining
forces to develop and expand a range of petrol
stations and distribution services.

The second part of the problem was to identify the
kind of name that reflected correctly the values and
aspirations of contemporary Argentina. Research
among target audiences revealed that a non-traditional
approach, focused on modernity, intelligence and
precision, would be the most acceptable. The result
was Eg3, a formula that signifies in Spanish 'the power
of three'. Thus the new name breaks with a tradition
of natural or energetic names for petrol, asserting a
positive attitude to the provision of quality and service,
and also reflecting the triumvirate structure of the
company.

The new identity has been launched as part of an
expansion drive, including the implementation of
cultural change programmes to develop organizational
behaviour in the wake of change.

- **Vitra GmbH**
  Weil am Rhein, Germany

  Identity for a furniture
  manufacturer

  1992

- Pierre Mendell

  Mendell & Oberer
  Munich, Germany

vitra.

Vitra manufacture furniture for offices, the public sector and the home market. The family-owned firm has a strong commitment to design, made visible not only in the ranges of furniture created for Vitra by world-class designers but also in their regular architectural commissions for new buildings, from architects such as Frank Gehry and Zaha Hadid. Their furniture, and their design achievement, has been regularly recognized with design awards.

Pierre Mendell, who created the current logo, acts as a consultant to Vitra on a wide range of areas. The simple but contemporary logo he created is only part of a design-based approach to their business on Vitra's part. Their architectural programme is described as 'corporate identity architecture', not in the thematic sense of repetitive structures but as visual evidence of their concern for a complete contemporary statement. Vitra takes the commonplace truism of 'design-led' and turns it into a true corporate theme.

Vitra logo (top) and Persona chairs (above),
designed by Mario Bellini. Photograph by Hans Hansen.

Zaha Hadid's Fire Station (left) and
Alvaro Siza's Manufacturing Centre
(below, left) at Weil am Rhein.
Photographs by Richard Bryant/Arcaid.

Meneba Meel
Rotterdam, The Netherlands

Logo and housestyle for merger
of two flour millers

1994

• Jos van der Zwaal, Dennis de Rond

Millford - Van Den Berg Design
Wassenaar, The Netherlands

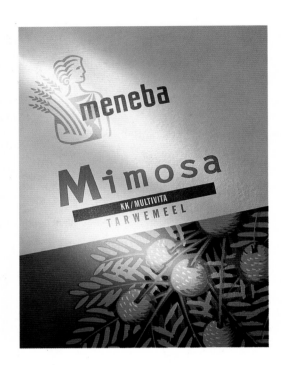

Meneba, one of the main suppliers in the Dutch flour market, itself part of the international Goodman Fielder group, recently took over Wessanen, to form a merged company controlling fifty-five percent of the market. Both companies had strong and loyal customer bases, and established staff traditions and procedures. The key themes of the new logo were leadership, friendship and expertise, and it is used on flour bags (over a range of eighty different items), bulk carriers and delivery vehicles, building signs and banners, and of course stationery and advertising. The introduction of the new identity was part of a broader programme to communicate the purposes of the new company to staff and customers, and recent research has shown that it has been very well accepted.

• **Deutsche Telekom**
Bonn, Germany

Revised identity for a telephone
company

1994

• Zintzmeyer & Lux
Zurich, Switzerland

Zintzmeyer & Lux have worked with Deutsche
Telekom, the German national telephone company,
on their corporate identity over the last few years,
but with the decision to privatize the service a new
identity was called for. The new identity, based on a
red serif capital T with white background and grey
detailing, is intended to smooth the transition from
public to private ownership.

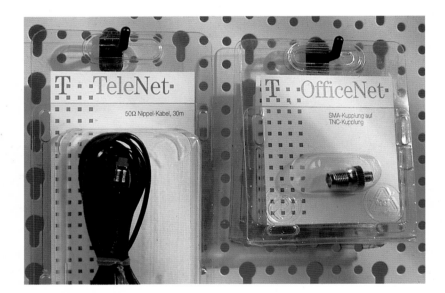

• **Axial Ltd.**
Barking, England

New name and identity following merger between two car transporting companies

1995

• Michael Denny, John Bateson,
Andrew Ross, Jeremy Roots, Michéle Bury

Roundel Design Group
London, England

The merger between Toleman Holding Company and Silcock Express within the Tibbett & Britten group created the largest new car delivery and pre-delivery inspection company in the UK: it needed a new name and identity. The name chosen was Axial, a conflation between axis and radial, and a virtual homophone for axle, all terms related to the automobile industry. The name also works well in the major European languages, where the new company also has a sizeable share of the market. The logo, a central point with radiating crescents, not only suggests stacked wheels but also reflects a night and day image of continuous service.

- **Telefónica**
Madrid, Spain

**New identity for the national
telephone company**

1994

- Joan Costa, Albert Culleré

CIAC
Barcelona, Spain

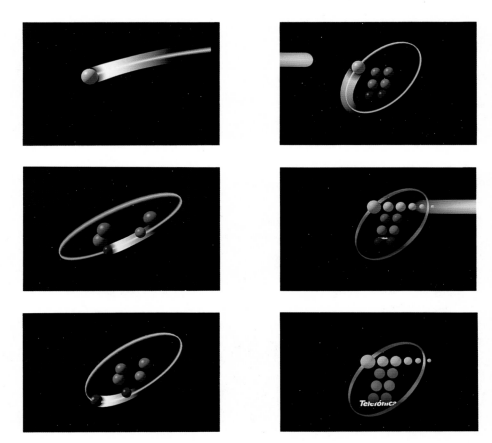

The new identity for Spain's national
telephone company evolves from
the previous one, and is redesigned
to emphasize the new technologies
of global telecommunication.

Sequence from a video presenting the new logo.

**• Cathay Pacific
Hong Kong**

**New identity for an international
airline**

1994

• Landor Associates
San Francisco, USA & Hong Kong

Cathay Pacific is a leading player in the highly competitive airline market in South-East Asia. While its green and white livery, introduced in the 1960s, is very well known, research inside and outside the company confirmed the management's view that change was called for, to coincide with the upgrading of the main fleet with Airbus and Boeing 777 aircraft.

The values that the new identity had to convey were the established professionalism, technical excellence and exacting standards of service for which the airline was renowned. Its Oriental heritage was also important. The decision to replace the green and white stripes with a brushwork bird's wing motif confirmed these values. It also repositioned the airline within the air travel language of the 21st century, less hard-hitting, not purely business-oriented, and instead suggestive of borderless international flight, like that of a migrating bird.

As part of the total package for repositioning the identity, ticket counters, signage, courtesy lounges and aircraft interiors were also redesigned. For interiors, in line with the main policy, a soothing water motif was adopted, in the green and blue tones of the new livery.

Landor Associates' first airline identity project was for Alitalia in 1969. Cathay Pacific joins a list of over thirty carriers who have benefitted from Landor's expertise in this field.

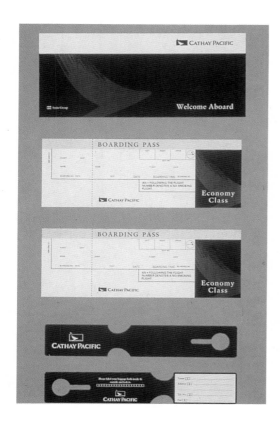

The new identity on the aircraft (facing) and on ticketing.

Customer services also benefit from the new identity,
with new interior design for reception facilities (above)
and airport lounges (facing).

• **Air Canada**
Toronto, Canada

**Identity and livery for a national
airline**

1994

• John Diefenbach

Diefenbach Elkins
San Francisco & New York, USA

The red maple leaf insignia of Air Canada may be one of the best
known in the airline world, but it has had its disadvantages. Many
Canadians assumed the familiar airline to be government-owned,
and so accorded it the poor estimation that they have for other
government services. In fact the airline was privatized in 1989.
A new identity was called for to make the break clear, without
losing the residual benefits of the old image.

Diefenbach Elkins began work on the new identity by
commissioning a broad-based survey of attitudes towards
Canada itself on the part of Canadians and others. The detailed
map of qualities such as hospitable, spacious, peaceful and
diverse that emerged as especially Canadian formed the
backdrop to the new approach. The familiar maple leaf has been
retained, but rendered more naturally on a deep green
background. A new element that is introduced is the Northern
Arc, a curved line symbolizing Canada's position at the top of
the globe.

These two devices are applied with a limited range of strong
colours (including the traditional red of the Canadian flag) to
aircraft liveries, signage, ticketing, reception areas and ground
vehicles. The launch of the new identity was also part of a major
programme of staff training. This was intended to emphasize the
change in the airline's status 'from civil service to customer
service'.

This excellent identity shows how it is possible to modify an
existing image, which had some negative associations, into a new
and positive one. The new image was firmly based in market
research, and executed in tandem with a campaign towards
employees to encourage the new values and perceptions of the
airline.

'The new look reflects Air Canada's strategy to be the airline
of Canada, the country and its people,' according to John
Diefenbach. For him, the work of the corporate identity
specialist 'is about identity not about image': discussion with
management, thorough research and planning are as important
as the graphic solution if an identity is to succeed.

• **Ferrovie dello Stato SpA
Rome, Italy**

**Corporate identity programme
for the Italian state and
international railway network**

1994

• Rob Davie, Vassoula Vasiliou

XMPR
London, England

Preliminary studies for the identity (above and
below) were finally developed into a curved sign with
a special alphabet (facing).

The decision to create a new corporate identity for the Italian
state railway company, Ferrovie dello Stato, coincided with a
period of dramatic political and economic change in Italy. The
dynamics of the change at the company were, however, internal.
The Ferrovie group not only operates a large rail network,
nationally and internationally, but is also involved in shipping,
property and finance. It is one of Italy's largest employers, and
has a customer base comprising millions of passengers each
year. Previously wholly State-controlled, it is moving into a
mixed, competitive economy.

Creating an identity for such a large and diverse organization,
with a keen sense of its own history and value, is a long-term
task, though shorter than that of implementing the chosen
design over hundreds of stations and thousands of locomotives,
carriages and rolling stock. This latter process will be completed
over a ten year period, as new stock is replaced or refurbished.
So the corporate identity is also being used as a validation mark
- stations, for example, will be re-badged after meeting new
policy standards, as well as after refurbishment.

The solution devised by XMPR International, based in London,
took two years of planning and consultation. It deliberately
retains and strengthens links with the past, and gives continuity,
individuality and scope to the different areas of operation of the
Ferrovie group. The result emphasizes the challenge faced by
designers in adapting an existing corporate identity to embrace
a new vision of the present and the future.

The new identity has three core elements: a logotype, a colour
scheme and a corporate alphabet. The identity programme
shows how these are to be applied to different areas within the
group, to different classes of train, to tickets, timetables,
uniforms and even ferryboats. The overall intention was to
create an identity that was softer and less harsh, more natural
and less mechanical, more entrepreneurial and less State-owned.
It would promote a company looking to the future with
judgement, balance and awareness.

The logotype or symbol was based on the letters FS, previously
used as the main label for the railways. However the letters are
now curved and stylized, linked to a fluid, forward motion
expressing both the transportational activity of the company and
its future vision.

ABCDEF
GHIJKLMN
OPQRSTU
VWXYZ&
1234567890

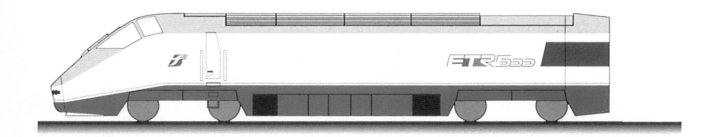

The new identity appears for the first time (above) on the high-speed train, while designs for other trains and for stations (facing) will be introduced gradually.

• **Eurostar**
Paris and London, Europe

Identity for high-speed train service

1994

• Minale Tattersfield Design Strategy
Richmond, Surrey, England and Paris, France

The Eurostar is the high-speed train linking London, Paris and Brussels through the tunnel under the English Channel. This high-profile and innovative project needed an image that would distinguish it from other train services in the countries it serves, as well as working internationally in all three. If the logo borrows from the ring of stars motif used by the European Union, it is so as to emphasize the centrally European role of the services, embodying the idea of a Europe without frontiers. The colour scheme of deep blue, yellow and greys is carried through from the exterior and the interior of the trains themselves, on to ticketing, catering material, timetables, uniforms and stationery.

• **Viva Air**
Madrid, Spain

Identity for a new charter airline

1992

• Daniel Panicello

CIAC
Barcelona, Spain

The new identity was created for Iberia, the Spanish flag-carrying airline, who were launching a new charter service for holidaymakers. The word 'viva' shouts Spain in any European language, and the bold graphics have a hand-painted feel, recalling the bold brushwork of modern Spanish art. The strong colours, redolent of sunshine and warmth, of the main logo are echoed in the interior colour scheme, but on a grey rather than a white background. The whole concept carries a basic message of vivid enjoyment.

The new identity (above right) and the seat patterning material (right), with the full livery for exteriors and interiors (facing).

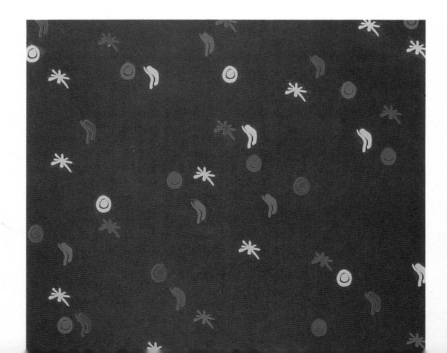

New Professions Manufacturing into service

The pattern of changes affecting large corporations and government agencies in the last two decades also had its effect on service industries. Deregulation of financial services and other professions, for example, created new opportunities, while the new complexities of corporate life called for the services of management consultants of all kinds. And the design profession itself grew both in numbers and skills.

To emphasize this shift from manufacturing to service, this section groups designers, consultancies, other professionals and those in print and paper. That designers would be eager to show off their skills on their own letterheads and cards is hardly surprising. What is interesting is how accountants, PR companies and management consultants have also turned to graphic designers to improve their images. An engineering company such as Owen Williams, for example, whose excellent letterhead by Roundel Design is shown in this section, might be expected to have a sufficient reputation on the basis of its completed work and proven design skills: the increment that an innovative and witty presentation could offer would at first sight appear quite small. But this ignores the increasing level of competition in all areas of business life, and the opportunities beyond design that the introduction of a new corporate identity offers. Putting a corporate identity into place, even in a small firm, means instructing staff in the use of the new stationery, and this can be the vehicle for restating the company's mission and reminding staff about the importance of client relations and the business's image. For no matter how good these relations are, improvement and refinement are always possible.

As the letterhead is often a primary aspect of corporate identity for small firms or professional groups, it provides a starting point for seeing how graphic design can be used to convey a complex message. The multi-part form/letter/invoice devised for their own use by the Dutch designers Studio Boot is a dynamic statement of their design approach, while Tel Design's use of colour in their work for Edburgh Consultants neatly emphasizes the division of the consultancy into two main service areas.

- **Gwen Baker
New York, USA**

**Personal stationery for a public
relations consultant**

1993

- Michael Gericke, Donna Ching

Pentagram Design
New York, USA

The letterhead makes a gentle pun on the client's name.

• **Neusch Architekten
St Gall, Switzerland**

**Letterhead for an architectural
practice**

1993

• Professor Michael Baviera

BBV
Zurich, Switzerland

archinüeschtekten

• **Joel Bénard**
Toronto, Canada

Stationery for a portrait
photographer

1992

• Paul Haslip

HM+E Incorporated
Toronto, Canada

**• Owen Williams Ltd
Birmingham, England**

**Corporate identity for a civil and
structural engineering company**

1994

• Michael Denny, John Bateson, Jonathan Simpson,
Rachel Dinnis, Harold Batten

Roundel Design Group
London, England

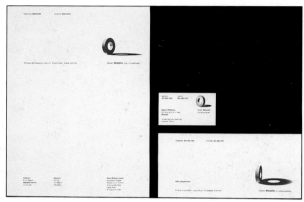

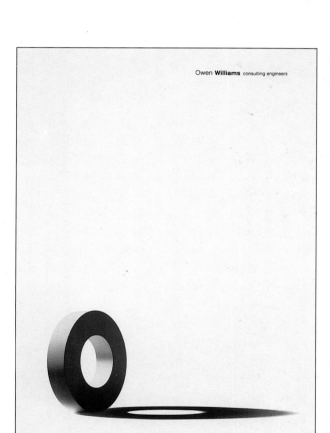

• Nijkamp & Nijboer
Oldenzaal, The Netherlands

**Stationery for a project
management business**

1994

• Gert Kootstra, Gitteke van der Linden

Tel Design
The Hague, The Netherlands

Nijkamp & Nijboer specialize in the implementation
of large corporate identity projects. Their own
corporate role is therefore in the background, and a
striking visual logo would have been inappropriate.
The solution was to combine a muted visual symbol
with the consistent use of a strong colour
combination.

• **Edburgh Consultants**
Utrecht, The Netherlands

**Stationery for a new educational
and informational management
company**

1994

• Gert Kootstra

Tel Design
The Hague, The Netherlands

097

New Professions

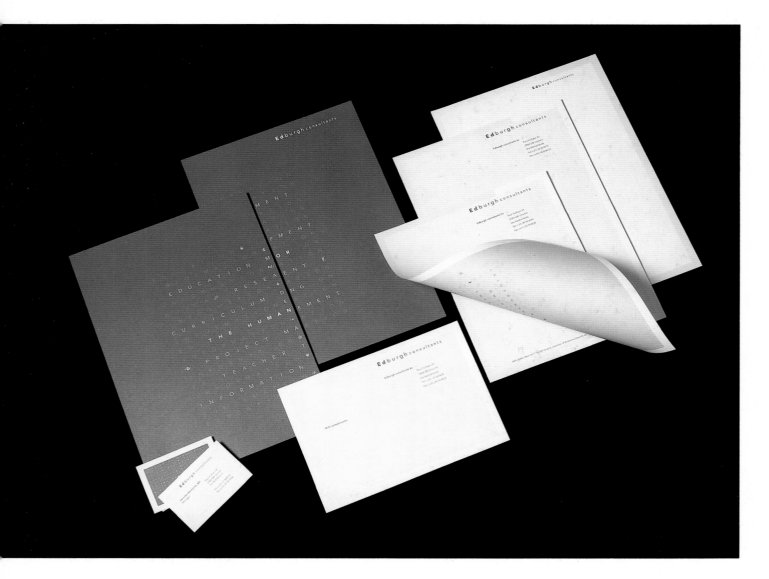

With the reorganization of the consultancy into two
divisions, a paired colour scheme and set of logos
were devised to emphasize the different but related
functions.

• Kemsley & Co.
Hildenborough, England

**Stationery for a small chartered
accountancy practice**

1993

• Martin Devlin, Brigid McMullen, Nina Jenkins

The Workroom
London, England

KEMSLEY +

AND CO =

CHARTERED •

ACCOUNTANTS •

KEMSLEY +
AND CO =
CHARTERED •
ACCOUNTANTS •

98a Tonbridge Road
Hildenborough, Kent TN11 9BT
Telephone (01732) 838381

98a Tonbridge Road
Hildenborough, Kent TN11 9BT
Telephone (01732) 838381

Robin Kemsley ACA ATII Consultant: Keith Sheehan

KEMSLEY +
AND CO =
CHARTERED •
ACCOUNTANTS •

98a Tonbridge Road
Hildenborough, Kent TN11 9BT
Telephone (01732) 838381
Robin Kemsley ACA ATII Consultant: Keith Sheehan

• **Blaich Associates**

Aspen, Colorado, USA
Identity for a design consultancy

1993

• Robert Blaich

Blaich Associates
Aspen, Colorado, USA

Designers' own logos pose a problem of discretion. Too weak an identity can give the impression of thin talent, while too strong a one can suggest energy expended in the wrong area. As Wally Olins commented, 'It's like your clients seeing you sitting in club class when they are walking down to economy seats.' Equally, a letterhead or visiting card can be the first visual contact a designer makes with a prospective client, and so needs to make a positive gesture. Many design consultancies, such as Siegel & Gale and Pentagram, rely on traditional typography, excellently composed, and strong primary colours.

Bob Blaich, former head of Corporate Industrial Design at Philips in Eindhoven, chose to make a more personal statement when he set up his own consultancy.

The large graphic capital B is based on his own signature.

Blaich Associates

Design Management Consultants

319 North Fourth Street
Aspen, 81611, Colorado, U.S.A.

Tel. 303 - 920 92 76
Fax 303 - 920 34 33

- **9-D Design**
  Zurich, Switzerland

  Identity for a design partnership

  1994

- Richard Feurer, Christian Hugin

  9-D Design
  Zurich, Switzerland

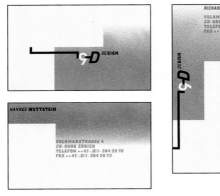

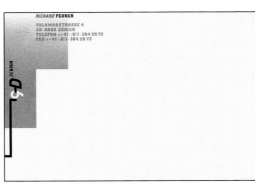

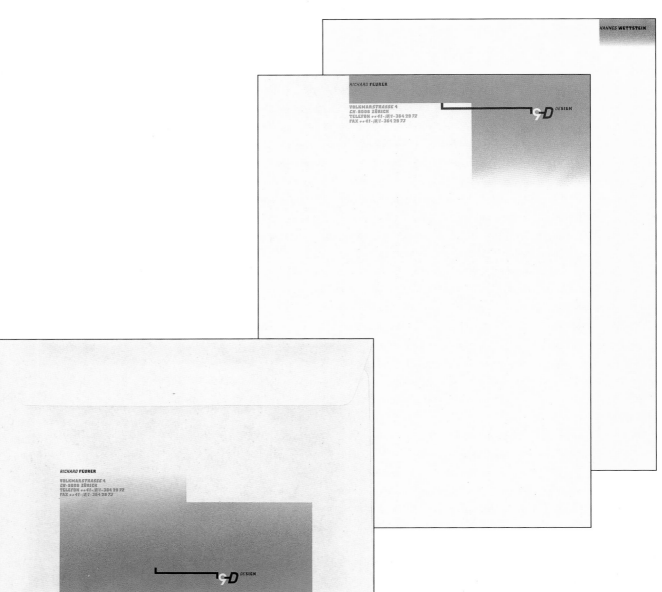

This single sheet unit is perforated, so that different elements can be omitted (for an invoice for example, the top righthand corner is applicable: remove this and you have a letterhead), or used independently (like the visiting card or compliments slip).

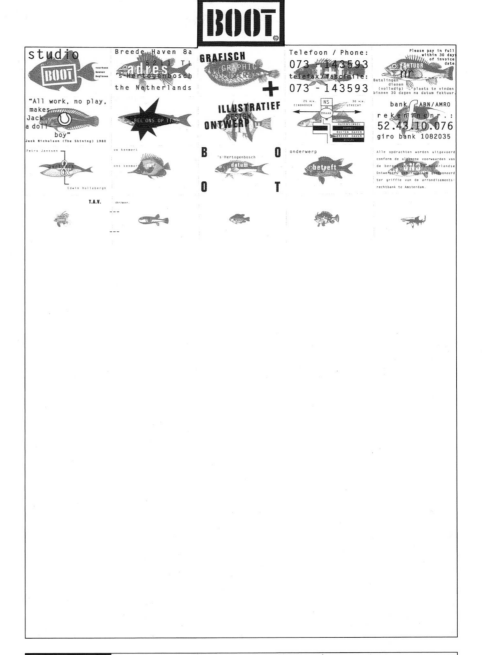

• Takeo Co., Ltd.
Tokyo, Japan

**Series of posters to promote an
annual paper exhibition**

1994

• Kenya Hara

Nippon Design Center, Inc.
Tokyo, Japan

The annual Takeo Paper World exhibition is a major
promotional event for the Takeo paper trading
company, and the themed posters an important part
of the company's public identity. The consistent
theme is texture, a traditional quality in paper.

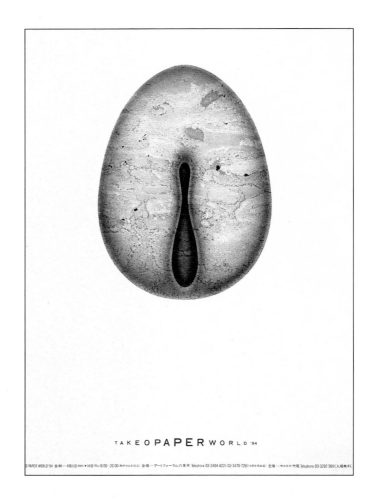

TAKEO PAPER WORLD '94

• Takeo Co., Ltd.
Tokyo, Japan

• Kenya Hara

Nippon Design Center, Inc.
Tokyo, Japan

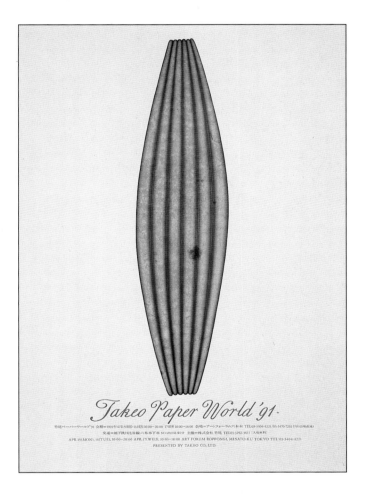

Takeo Paper World '91

竹尾ペーパーワールド'91 会期■1991年4月15日(MON)-16日(火)10:00～20:00 17日(水) 10:00～18:00 会場■アート・フォーラム六本木 TEL.03-3404-4221/03-3470-7261 (90会場直通)
交通■地下鉄日比谷線六本木下車 NO.4出口徒歩5分 主催■株式会社 竹尾 TEL.03-3292-3611 「入場無料」
APR.15(MON), 16(TUE), 10:00～20:00 APR.17(WED), 10:00～18:00 ART FORUM ROPPONGI, MINATO-KU TOKYO TEL.03-3404-4221
PRESENTED BY TAKEO CO.,LTD.

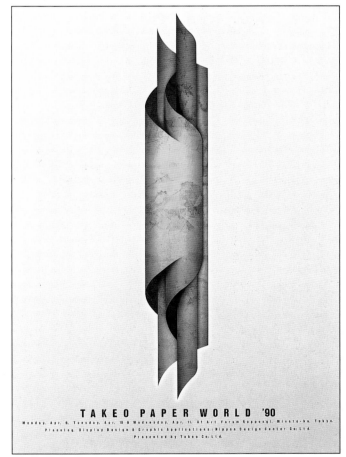

TAKEO PAPER WORLD '90

Monday, Apr. 9, Tuesday, Apr. 10 & Wednesday, Apr. 11. At Art Forum Roppongi, Minato-ku, Tokyo.
Planning, Display Design & Graphic Applications: Nippon Design Center Co. Ltd.
Presented by Takeo Co. Ltd.

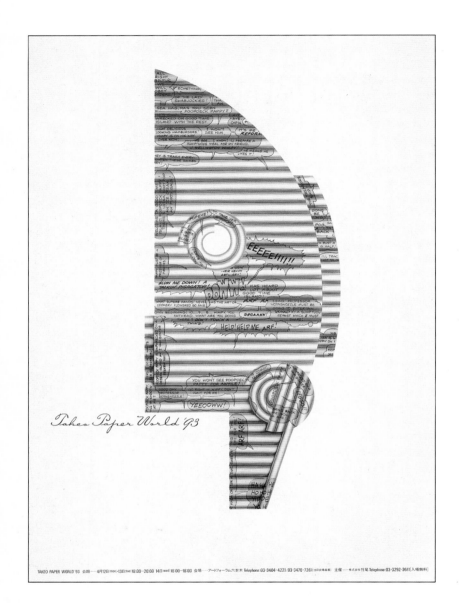

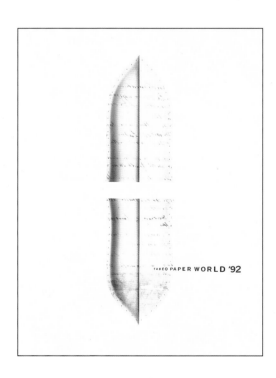

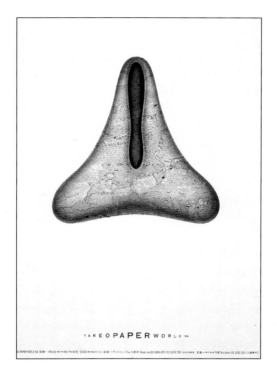

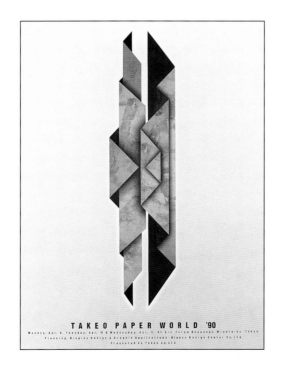

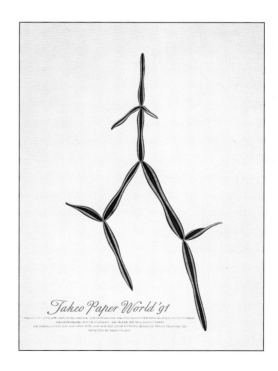

• **Champion Paper
New York, USA**

**Promotional identity for paper
manufacturer**

1992

• Woody Pirtle, John Klotnia

Pentagram Design
New York, USA

Kromekote is a range of papers featuring a
high-gloss surface. To symbolize this
reflective character, the design is based on
a capital letter 'K' made up from the top
half of the letter and its mirror image,
continuously repeated.

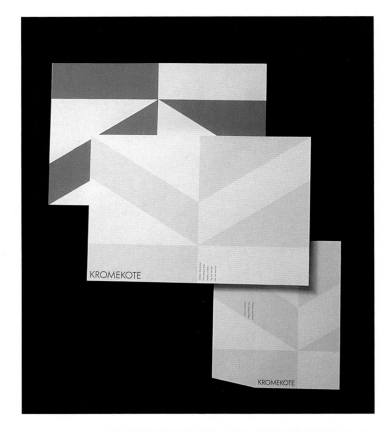

· Connect Colour Litho Ltd.
Hemel Hempstead, England

Identity for a printing firm

1994

· Matthew Frost

The Team
London, England

107 New Professions

Connect Colour Litho
Avebury House
6 Avebury Court
Hemel Hempstead
Hertfordshire HP2 7TA

T 0442 69788
F 0442 211686

Date

Connect Colour Litho
Avebury House
6 Avebury Court
Hemel Hempstead
Hertfordshire HP2 7TA

T 0442 69788
F 0442 211686

Ian Butler
Director

Connect Colour Litho Limited, Registered Office: Avebury House, 6 Avebury Court, Hemel Hempstead, Hertfordshire HP2 7TA. Registered in England No: 2243880

• **Benders Ltd.**
London, England

Identity for paper products
manufacturer

1993

• The Partners
London, England

Benders manufacture a wide range of paper products
and disposables. Many of these, such as the paper
doillies for drinks used by British Airways, carry
the client's own name or logo, but Benders felt that
a new identity would help conserve their leading
position in the market and bring their services more
clearly to the attention of clients.

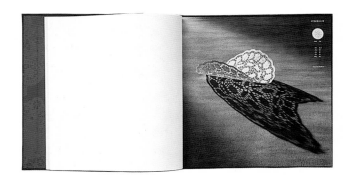

• **Bolt & Nuts Studio**
Yokohama, Japan

Identity for a graphic design
company

1992

• Kenzo Nakagawa

Bolt & Nuts Studio
Yokohama, Japan

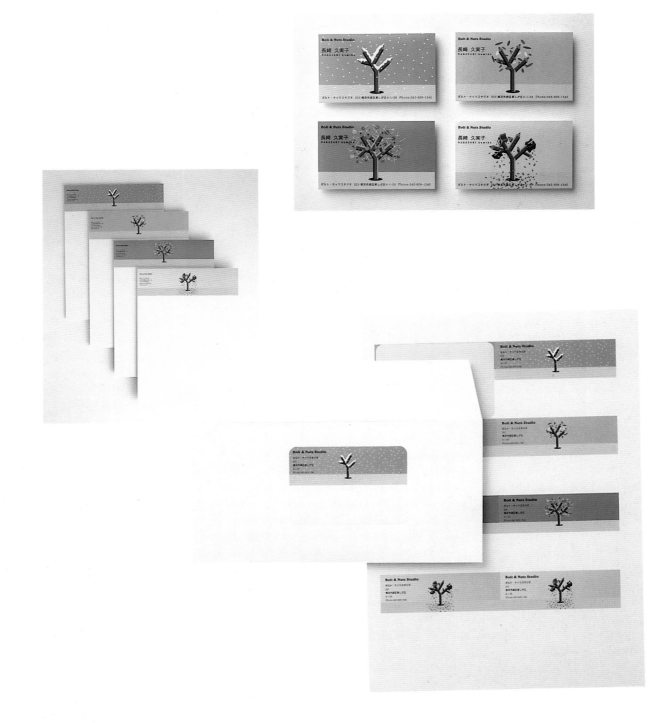

New Technologies Working the infobahn

Wally Olins in his introduction highlights the importance of technology as one of the factors of change in the world of corporate identity, particularly in respect of the presentation of the corporate image on-screen or via electronic media. This section looks at some of the companies whose area of business lies in the field of new technologies, particularly electronics, communications and biotechnology.

The few on-screen identities submitted for this book created problems of definition: is a TV station ident an example of true corporate identity, or solely of branding, for example? And where the presentation of the station identity is changed from season to season, how do we draw the line between a corporate identity programme and an advertising exercise? Or are we seeing the start of a new form, one entirely *sui generis*? With the increasing use of electronic media, these questions will have to be answered, or more likely, our definitions of corporate identity modified, away from a perception based on the application of graphic solutions, in favour of corporate identity as an activity.

In this functional sense, corporate identity becomes a continuous process of evaluating and presenting the company, in which the traditional elements of signage, logo, letterhead and manual will be joined by advertising, staff training, architecture, client relations, and market and product research. In an intensely competitive market, this process, as we have seen, is already beginning to take hold in the best companies. It is a process that the opportunities and challenges offered by technology must encourage. The opportunities are the increasing possibilities of bringing the corporation to the attention of its constituents, in different, primarily visual, ways. The challenges lie in the risks of information overload in a world where hundreds of different agencies - television and cable channels, video and CD-Rom, Internets and infobahns - will be competing for the consumer's attention. The task for the corporate identity designer and manager will be to maintain the visibility of the company in this new situation.

• **FM802**
Osaka, Japan

**Identity and supporting materials
for a radio station**

1990

• K2
Tokyo, Japan

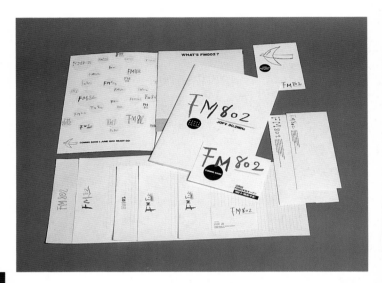

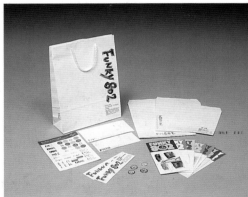

The growth of FM radio stations worldwide is a recent phenomenon: according to some industry specialists, radio advertising is going to be a major medium for the 1990s. The expansion of services is partly due to improved technology, and partly to a general redistribution of frequencies that has freed up the airwaves. This expansion has fed in turn competition for listeners, particularly teenagers and young adults. And since a radio station's identity is largely aural, any visual element that can bolster listener perceptions is useful: Tshirts, carrier bags, stickers and showcards, such as those designed here by K2 for a Japanese client.

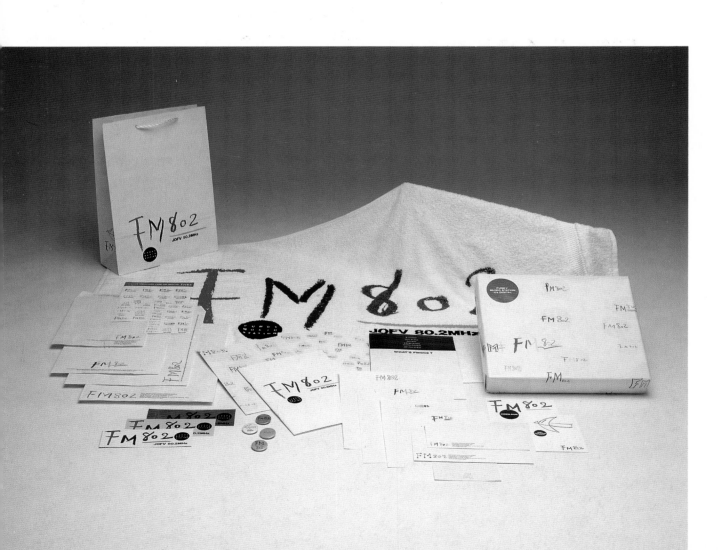

• **Westminster Cable**
London, England

Identity for a cable television company

1994

• Stephen Franks, Simon Carter

Coley Porter Bell
London, England

Cable television is a growth business in the UK, and Westminster Cable, with a franchise in the heart of London, were well placed in the market. But some potential customers linked the name and former logo with the municipal authority, and so a new identity was designed to link the service with the exciting, busy atmosphere of the area. It uses as a logo a capital W that echoes time-lapsed photographs of moving car lights, and the background images for advertising and publications feature lively street scenes from Westminster.

• **Westminster Cable**
London, England

**Starwave Corporation
Bellevue, USA**

**Logo and identity for an
information technology company**

1992

Jack Anderson, Denise Weir, Lian Ng,
David Bates

Hornall Anderson Design Works
Seattle, USA

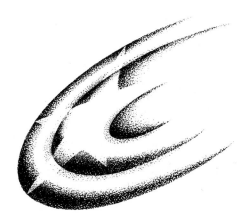

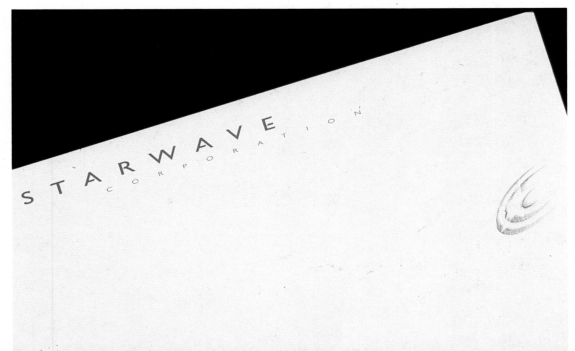

• **Production House**
Hamburg, Germany

**Identity for a video production
studio**

1993

• Peter Schmidt

Peter Schmidt Design
Hamburg, Germany

**• Pathogenesis
New York, USA**

**Identity and mark for a
biotechnology company**

1992

• Woody Pirtle, John Klotnia

Pentagram Design
New York, USA

117 New Technologies

Pathogenesis is a biotechnology company formed to specialize in the diagnosis and treatment of bacterial and viral infections. They aim to identify pathogens, the source of disease. Pentagram designed a corporate symbol to communicate this mission visually. When the company put forward its initial public offering in 1992 it raised $41 million from investors including Bill Gates of MicroSoft and one of the world's largest healthcare companies, Baxter International Inc.

PATHOGENESIS

- **Aetypos**
  Utrecht, The Netherlands

  **New identity for a consultancy
  following reorganization**

  1994

- Gert Kootstra, Gitteke van der Linden

  Tel Design
  The Hague, The Netherlands

The two new sections of the consultancy are distinguished
by separate colour codings, and united by the dolphin motif
and matching typographic styles.

• **NBN**
Sydney, Australia

**Vehicle livery for a news
broadcasting unit**

1993

• Raphael Klaesi

One Ahead Graphic Design Studio
St Ives, NSW, Australia

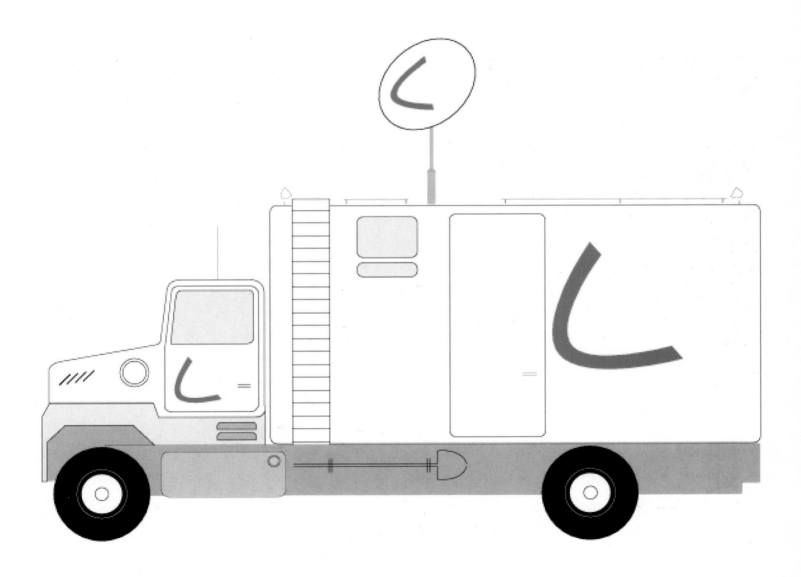

• NBN
Sydney, Australia

Vehicle livery for a news
broadcasting unit

Raphael Klaesi

One Ahead Graphic Design Studio
St Ives, NSW, Australia

New Lifestyles Modes for a millennium

The consumer explosion of the 1980s has been decried as a time of waste and excess, ending in recession and economic decline. But the design energy that went into those years has left a permanent legacy in the shape of better shop and restaurant design, keener packaging, and more product choice. Designers still play an important role in giving this continuing change material form, and identity has been particularly recognized in the retail market as a valuable tool in reaching and keeping customers. So this section begins with a range of new designs for restaurants, shops and retail goods. These show how the retail market has itself developed new marketing strategies, through designer shops such as the Nicole Farhi store in London, with an identity designed by Din Graphics to specialist outlets such as Starlite Dance (designed by Lewis Moberly).

As the consumer market took up the greater use of corporate design, other organizations equally concerned with reaching a wide public began to follow suit. Charitable bodies are a typical example: they need to make a strong case to the public for support, and be clearly identified among decision makers - whether corporate givers, the press, politicians or public servants - as part of their lobbying and organizational functioning. Some years ago it used to be said that design consultancies needed to do work for charities - often for free - to prove their serious status, but today charities are as professional in their approach to design as other clients, and appreciate the value of quality corporate design. The Partners' recent work for Mencap, a charity defending the interests of the mentally handicapped, is a case in point: Mencap were looking for an image with a broader appeal than their previous logo, one aimed at gaining positive support rather than only evoking sympathy, and the new identity has the aptness and rigour necessary for such a brief. Other organizations in the health field have also turned to corporate identity to strengthen their position, particularly in the new market for healthcare in Britain.

Cultural institutions have followed the same path: this was partly in response to finding new sources of funding, and much more in response to an appreciation of the changing role of culture in society. Museums are no longer seen as silent treasure houses, but as active participants in public education and leisure. The redesign of the Louvre Museum in Paris began with I.M. Pei's dramatic glass pyramid, and has continued through the opening of the Richelieu Wing (also designed by Pei) into a new identity as Le Grand Louvre, where the posters, ticketing, publications and even the shopping bags extend a welcome to the visitor that cannot be compared to the earlier public face of the museum.

The integration in their approach to the public has led us to group traditional retailers, restaurants and consumer goods with the new generation of charitable, cultural and sports activities found in this section. There has been some debate about the appropriateness of charitable and cultural bodies pursuing the consumer so commercially ('the museum shop is bigger than the exhibition space' was such a comment I once heard). That political argument does not concern us here: rather we wish to show that the best graphic and corporate identity design can serve the needs of many different lifestyle organizations.

**• Orient Tea Room
Hong Kong**

Identity for a restaurant

1992

• Alan Chan, Philip Leung

Alan Chan Design Co.
Wanchai, Hong Kong

The design of restaurant interiors, fittings, cutlery and
identities has been a growth area in Europe over the last
decade and more. The increasing sophistication of the city
of Hong Kong, and its growing importance as a business
and tourist centre has led to a parallel expansion there.
Alan Chan's designs for this 'tea room' match the traditions
of Oriental cuisine with the equally demanding but different
standards of Western taste.

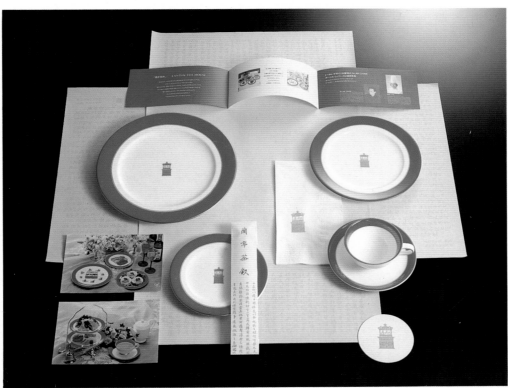

• **Nicole's**
London, England

New identity for a restaurant

1993

• Valerie Wickes, Laura Price

Din Graphics
London, England

Nicole's is a new restaurant within the Nicole Farhi clothes shop in New Bond Street, London. Din Graphics were involved with design for the new Black on Black collection, and were invited to work on menus, signage and decor for the restaurant as well. The restaurant offers a range of simple, mainly Continental dishes, and the design aim was for a matching classical, simple setting.

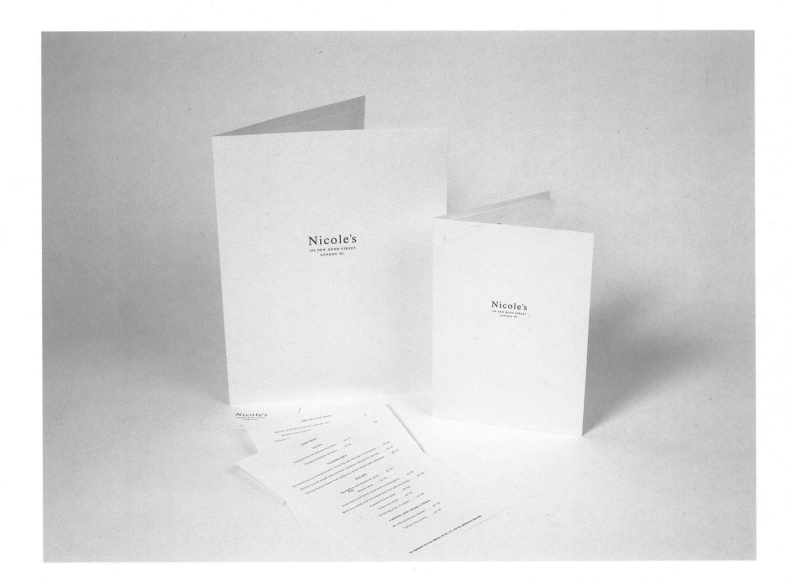

• **The Good Diner**
New York, USA

Name, signage and interior
for a new restaurant

1992

• Michael Bierut, Woody Pirtle, Lisa Cerveny,
James Biber

Pentagram Design
New York, USA

Gotham Equities' first real-estate development venture
was a restaurant on a 3,000 square foot site on 42nd
Street in New York. Pentagram were asked to name the
restaurant, and design the logo and the interior decoration.
The name 'The Good Diner' was chosen for its directness,
and portrayed through the logo of a coffee cup with halo.
The interior fittings were chosen to reflect the vernacular
traditions of American diners, with simple shapes and
strong colours, while the mural decorations, also designed
by Pentagram, are huge framed photocopies of archetypal
diner objects such as cruets, cups and teabags. A casual,
unpretentious atmosphere was the desired result of this
approach. The restaurant design has won awards from
the American Institute of Graphic Arts, the Art Directors
Club, and *Print* and *Communications Arts* magazines.

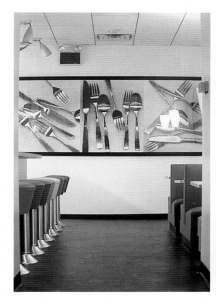

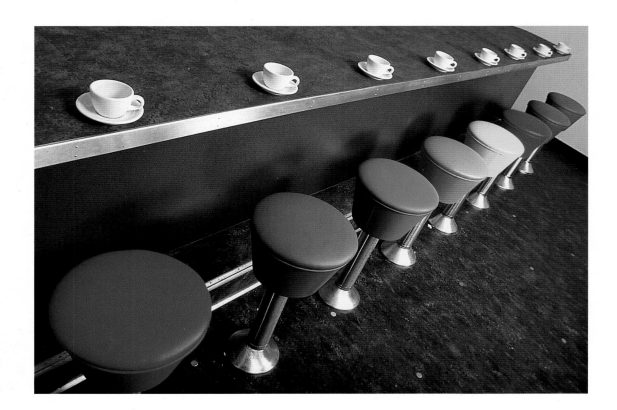

• **Chelsea Lighting Design**
London, England

Identity for a lighting retailer

1991/2

• Martin Devlin, Brigid McMullen, Analiese Cairis

The Workroom
London, England

This new outlet for lighting aims to sell design and fittings to both the architectural and the domestic markets for lighting. An overly technical approach would not have been appropriate, and so the designers opted for the metaphor of hand shadows to convey the aim of skill in achieving lighting effects that is the company's central purpose.

• **Horai Co., Ltd.**
Tokyo, Japan

Identity and packaging for a
manufacturer of dairy products

1992

• Hiroshi Kojitani, Kensuke Irie, Akira Seto

Kojitani, Irie & Inc.
Tokyo, Japan

• **Kohga Communication Products**
Tokyo, Japan

Identity and stationery for a
publishing company

1993

• Kenzo Nakagawa

Bolt & Nuts Studio
Tokyo, Japan

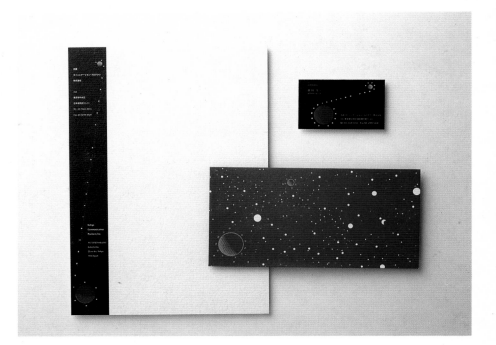

- **Spaghetti Recordings**
  London, England

  **Corporate identity and branding
  for a new record company**

  1992

- David Hillman, Karin Beck

  Pentagram Design Ltd.
  London, England

Spaghetti is a record label set up by Tennant and Lowe of The Pet Shop Boys for young, unknown artists. Pentagram created a design based on the word spaghetti set in elongated, condensed sans serif capitals, a visual pun on a strand of spaghetti. This could be used horizontally or vertically, or run around the side of a record cover: its flexibility was an essential part of the design.

Cicero
with Sylvia Mason-James
Live For Today

• **The Mandarin Flower Shop
Hong Kong**

Identity for in-hotel flower shop

1993

• Alan Chan, Chen Shun Tsoi

Alan Chan Design Co.
Wanchai, Hong Kong

• **Nicole Farhi**
Barking, England

New collection for a fashion
designer/retailer

1994

• Valerie Wickes, Laura Price

Din Graphics
London, England

• **Hugo Boss
Metzingen, Germany**

**Linked brands and corporate
identity for a fashion retailer**

1993

• Peter Schmidt

Peter Schmidt Design
Berlin, Germany

Fashion labels are valuable and important properties, and their use needs
to be carefully monitored to ensure market success. With three clothing
brands in the Hugo Boss stable, Boss, Hugo and Baldessarini, Peter
Schmidt was invited to produce an identity manual and master designs to
control the single and mixed use of the designs.

- **Starlite Dance**
  Sleaford, England

  Identity for specialist mail-order
  retailer of dancewear

  1993

- Lewis Moberly
  London, England

Starlite Dance is a small company in the north of England selling dancewear of all kinds, mainly by mail order via dance teachers, who in turn sell the products on to their pupils.

The standard image for dancewear is the ballerina. But today that wholly fails to reflect the range of dance styles taught or the aspirations of teachers and students. Lewis Moberly instead provided a visual interpretation of the company name - a star in the spotlight - with a series of abstract and lively images that transcend barriers of age, sex and dance style. The design has been carefully developed to be applicable across brochures, packaging and advertising, and to print in monochrome or colour.

The Starlite Dance identity won awards in 1994 from *Design Week,* and the New York Art Directors Club. It was a finalist in the Design Business Association Design Effectiveness Awards.

Starlite Dance

UNIT 2, HOGS BARN
SCREVINGTON
SLEAFORD
LINCOLNSHIRE
NG34 0AB

TELEPHONE 0529 306346
FACSIMILE 0529 306396

Starlite Dance

- **Tower Shop
Yokohama, Japan**

  **Identity and stationery for a
souvenir shop in the Landmark
Tower, Yokohama**

  1993

- Kenzo Nakagawa

  NDC Graphics
Tokyo, Japan

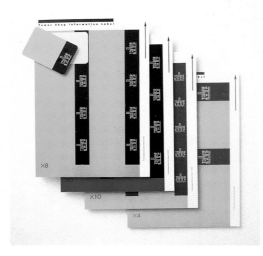

• **Our Price Music Ltd.**
London, England

**Logotype, signage and point
of sale material for home
entertainment retailer**

1993

• Nicholas Thirkell, Iain Crockart

CDT Design Ltd.
London, England

Our Price's former identity was shown by market
research to be 'dull, boring and drab': it featured a
white vinyl record in a red frame. CDT substituted a
CD, while retaining the red and white colour scheme
and modernizing the typography. At the same time the
shop interiors were remodelled to create a less
confusing environment, with new racking, signage,
labelling, shopping bags and staff shirts. The result was
a 6% increase in sales volume, like for like over six
months, and greater customer perception of the
company's shops as 'up to the minute'.

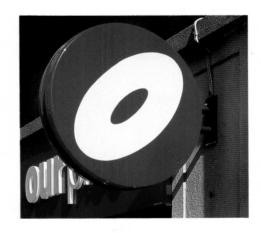

• Adelphi Distillery
Edinburgh, Scotland

Identity and packaging for a
Scotch whisky broker

1993

• Graham Scott, Julie Hampton

McIlroy Coates Ltd.
Edinburgh, Scotland

Unlike wine, which needs to be bottled in coloured glass to prevent discoloration, whisky is not susceptible to light, and can be bottled in plain glass. This fact was put to good use in creating a cost-effective but distinct identity for a specialist supplier of rare, quality malt whiskies.

Adelphi purchase individual casks of selected whiskies, and bottle and sell them under their own label. Each cask only produces a finite number of bottles, and is in effect a limited edition, though competitively priced. By the use of a small label, colour-coded to the main whisky-producing areas of Scotland, the connoisseur has the quality of the product, its colour and clarity, in full view. This direct but discerning approach is supported by the choice of simple pulpboard packaging, deliberately distancing Adelphi whiskies from other, over-packaged brands.

• **Komatsu Ginza**
Tokyo, Japan

Identity for a luxury
department store

1990

• K2
Tokyo, Japan

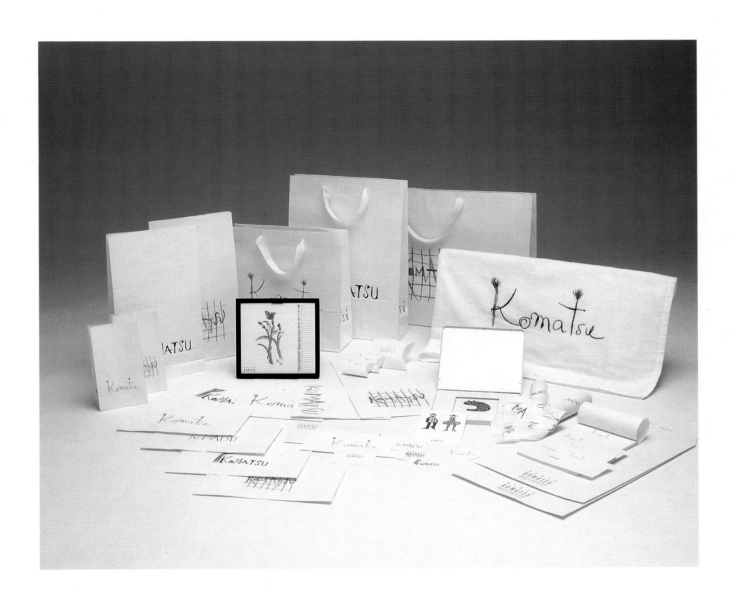

• Workers' Educational Association
London, England

New identity for an educational association

1994

• Philip Wong

Carter Wong & Partners
London, England

The WEA has a distinguished history in providing educational opportunities and support for working people. The change from a name to an acronym offered the opportunity to restate the association's serious and long-established purpose, to give it more visible presence in the continuing competition for funding, and to maintain the status of the regional divisions.

SOUTH EASTERN DISTRICT

YORKSHIRE SOUTH DISTRICT

CHESHIRE MERSEYSIDE
WEST LANCASHIRE DISTRICT

WORKING FOR
EDUCATIONAL ADVANCE

NORTH WESTERN DISTRICT

WORKING FOR
EDUCATIONAL ADVANCE

EASTERN DISTRICT

WORKING FOR
EDUCATIONAL ADVANCE

YORKSHIRE NORTH DISTRICT

EASTERN DISTRICT

SCOTLAND

● **International Centre against
Censorship
London, England**

**Corporate identity for a pressure
group**

1992

● David Hillman

Pentagram Design Ltd.
London, England

The Centre was set up to defend Article Nineteen
of the Universal Declaration of Human Rights, which
establishes the 'right to freedom of opinion and
expression'. The logo is based on the roman numeral
for nineteen.

- **Zjaak**
Rotterdam, The Netherlands

**Corporate identity and signage
for a community centre**

1993

- Paul Vermijs

Tel Design
The Hague, The Netherlands

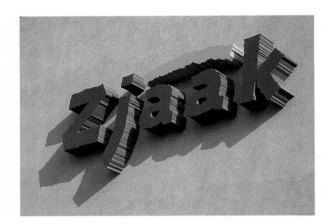

Zjaak is a community centre in a new housing
development in Rotterdam. The centre offers a full
range of services, including theatre, cinema, library,
and meeting rooms for local groups. The word Zjaak
means Jack, and reflects the down to earth directness
of the people of Rotterdam. The open and informal
lettering was chosen to reflect this, and is carried
through on to the pictograms used for signage
(designed by Marcel Groenen). Part of the brief was
to create a logo and signage that would not restrict
the attitude and activity of the centre, but would
rather evolve with the needs and demands of its
constituents.

vergaderruimte

• **Silvanus Trust
Launceston, England**

Corporate identity for a charity

1992

• Lewis Moberly Ltd.
London, England

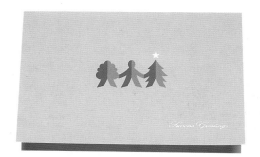

The Silvanus Trust has been set up to help preserve
small woodlands, through direct stewardship and
with advice and information. These two aspects
needed to be united in the logo, which stresses the
theme of partnership.

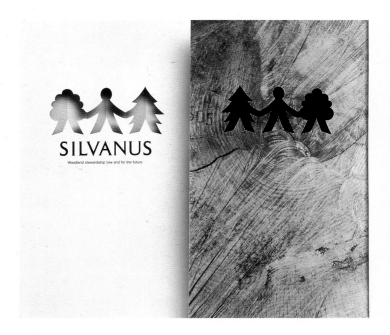

Contents

- **Victim Support**
  London, England

  Identity for a support group

  1993

- Valerie Wickes, Laura Price

  Din Graphics
  London, England

Victim Support was set up to help the victims of violent crime recover from the difficulties they had suffered. It is in many ways a new kind of charity, not linked to specific sections of the population nor to specific maladies. Research suggests that one of the main problems victims face is finding someone aware and sympathetic to talk to, and the courage to discuss a traumatic episode in their lives. The poster campaign was designed to catch the attention of the public by personalizing the role of victim through direct narration, and so also emphasize that help is available. This strong and direct approach has been most successful in heightening general awareness of the plight of victims of crime.

• **Mencap**
London, England

Corporate identity for a charity
for the mentally handicapped

1993

• The Partners
London, England

If attitudes of charities towards identity have changed
in the last decade, so have public attitudes towards
the mentally handicapped. Mencap, a leading British
charity and pressure group, wished to reposition its
identity away from the 'sad little Stephen' logo of the
past towards a positive image of the handicapped as
having a full and proper role in society, whether
young or old, and of whatever ethnic background.
The new series of images is also simply structured,
with a set of guidelines for use which are deliberately
cost-effective.

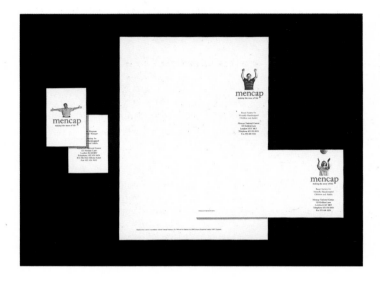

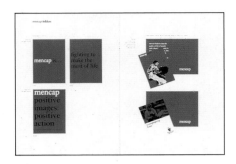

• **London Clinic for Fertility
London, England**

Identity for a gynaecological clinic

1993

• The Team
London, England

This identity for a new clinic specializing in gynaecology uses a simple, classical image combined with excellent typography and careful choice of paper to create an image that is both elegant and reassuring.

THE LONDON FERTILITY & GYNAECOLOGY CENTRE

PROFESSOR IAN CRAFT FRCS FRCOG
DIRECTOR

COZENS HOUSE 112A HARLEY STREET LONDON W1N 1AF
TELEPHONE 071 224 0707 FAX 071 224 3102

THE LONDON FERTILITY & GYNAECOLOGY CENTRE
DIRECTOR PROFESSOR IAN CRAFT FRCS FRCOG   DEPUTY DIRECTOR MR. TALHA AL-SHAWAF FRCS MRCOG

COZENS HOUSE 112A HARLEY STREET LONDON W1N 1AF TELEPHONE 071 224 0707 FAX 071 224 3102
ASSOCIATES MR. RIFKY GUIRGIS MRCOG MR. RAJIV RANGRASS MRCOG
MR. ALEX TSAKIRIS MRCOG DR. SUADAD SHAKIR FRABCS
REGISTERED IN ENGLAND NO 1604589 REGISTERED OFFICE CHAPEL HOUSE 24 NUTFORD HOUSE LONDON W1H 6AE

• **Royal Hospital for Neuro-Disability**
London, England

Corporate identity for a specialist hospital

1994

• Pierre Vermeir, Jim Sutherland, John Grey

Halpin Grey Vermeir
London, England

With the reorganization of the National Health Service in Britain a number of hospitals acquired a new status and many new roles. In the case of the former Royal Hospital and Home, in Putney, the hospital became the leading national centre for the care of severe neuro-disabilities. The simple and direct new logo suggests hope after darkness: it is in two basic colours which are also used in signage, on flags and uniforms, as well as on stationery.

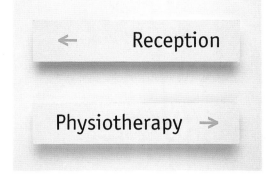

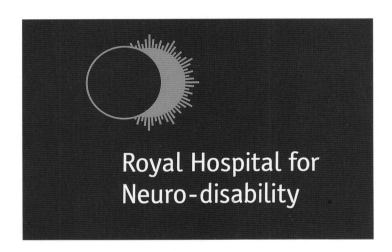

• **Museo d'Arte Moderna**
Lugano, Italy

Stationery and publications for a
museum of modern art

1992

• Daniele Garbarino, Maurice Hoderas

Studio Grafico Garbarino Hoderas
Carabietta, Switzerland

M
d'A
M

Museo
d'Arte
Moderna

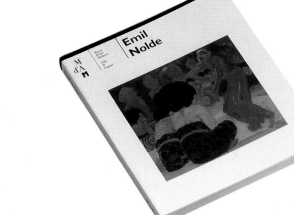

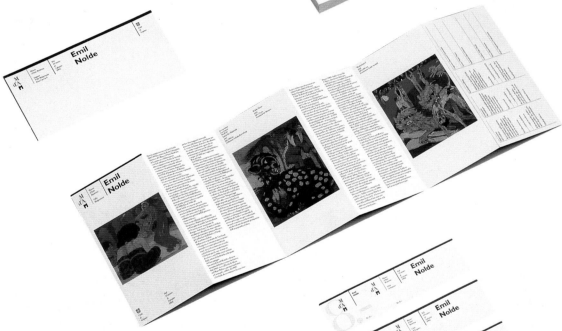

In 1992 the city of Lugano decided to rename its art gallery, used for exhibitions of modern and contemporary art. The designers created a logotype/mark based on the initial letters of the new name, including the *d'*. The mark uses Bodoni and Gill, to represent the nineteenth century origins and the twentieth century fields of activity of the museum. The mark forms the basis for a modular typographic system, with a strict grid. Exhibition materials are printed on white paper, different administrative forms on different coloured papers. Posters and advertising banners follow the same rules and hierarchy of design.

• **CBK Dordrecht
Dordrecht, The Netherlands**

**Stationery, posters, invitations,
catalogues for a contemporary art
gallery**

1993-4

• Wout de Vringer

Faydherbe/de Vringer
The Hague, The Netherlands

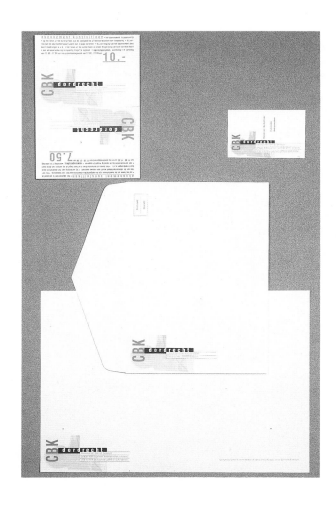

The CBK presents a regular series of exhibitions of
contemporary art, by a wide range of artists. At the
same time it is engaged, as are many galleries and
museums, in attracting a regular audience and looking
for corporate sponsorship. The challenge for Wout
de Vringer was to devise an approach that would not
be too restrictive but would be coherent. He chose
not to establish a fixed set of rules but to allow the
design for each exhibition to evolve from the work
shown: 'a corporate identity in a broad sense', as he
puts it, in which a continuing thread of style would
enable the public to recognize the work as being for
and about CBK.

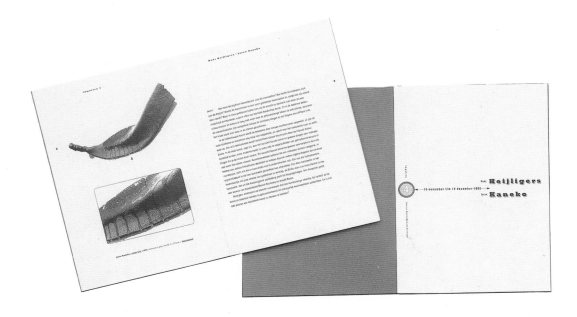

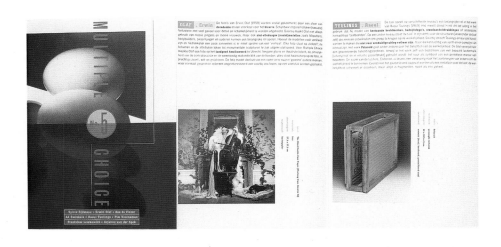

• **Musée d'art moderne et contemporain de Genéve Geneva, Switzerland**

Corporate identity including signage for new arts centre

1993

• Ruedi Baur, Denis Coueignoux, Eva Kubinyi

Ruedi Baur et Associés
Montreuil - Paris, France

Corporate symbol

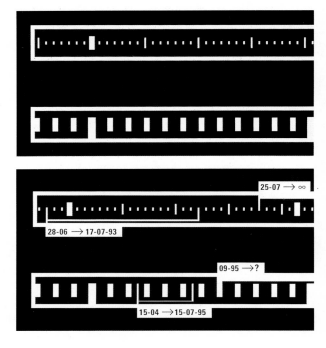

Time, extent and duration are frequent pre-occupations of contemporary art, according to Christian Bernard, the director of this new space for temporary exhibitions and events in Geneva. The identity picks up on this theme, using a ruler either as a carrier for the museum's name in Univers condensed lower case type, or as a marker for dates or headings. The gradations on the bar are consciously left unidentified; whether they serve to mark space or time, and in what units, is either open or can be specified by annotation.

A metallic grey green is used as the key colour. This deliberately industrial tint, together with the mechanical device of the ruler, reflects the fact that the museum is in a converted factory, and retains the feeling of a working space. This duality - on industry and time, work and duration - remains a strong theme. The sponsorship leaflet, for example, has a front cover made of copper, a durable material which in time patinates into the colour of the museum's type, and a back cover in corrugated cardboard, naturally biodegradable.

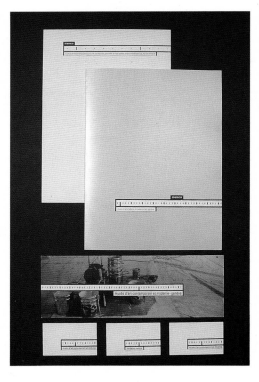

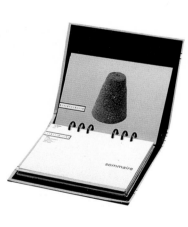

Corporate manual

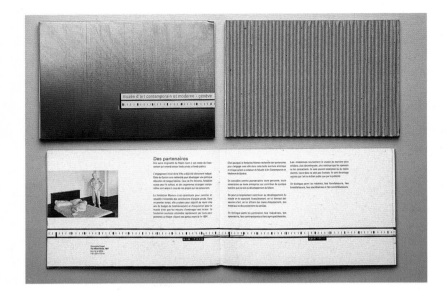

Museum catalogue

Poster

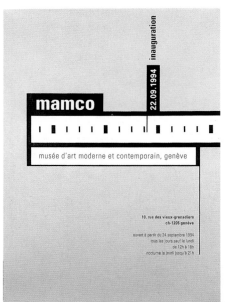

Series of posters for exhibitions.

• **Geffrye Museum**
London, England

Identity for museum of interiors

1993

• Lewis Moberly
London, England

GEFFRYE MUSEUM

The Geffrye Museum in the East End of London is dedicated to the study of domestic life in London's history. The displays are in effect 'room sets', showing typical interiors from different periods. When the museum achieved independent status, a new identity was called for, and the design solution uses the apt metaphor of the keyhole, encouraging the visitor to discover the world of the past.

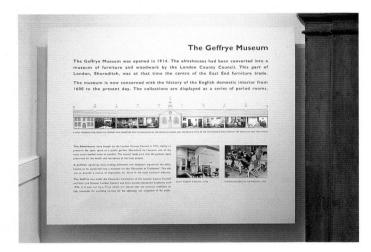

• **Royal Armouries**
Leeds, England

New logo and signage for museum
of historic armours and weapons

1994

• Minale Tattersfield & Partners
Richmond, Surrey, England

ROYAL ARMOURIES MUSEUM

ORIENTAL

HUNTING

The central logo for the Royal Armouries
is based on a design for a sixteenth-century
jousting helmet: it will not be seen officially
in place until the museum opens in its
new home in Leeds in the year 2000.
The decision to begin the new identity work
so early was taken in order to maintain
a continuity of interest in the collection
(formerly housed in the Tower of London)
during the creation of the new museum.

TOURNAMENT

FRIENDS OF THE MUSEUM

• **Euromusico**
Rome, Italy

Identity for a non-profit musical and cultural association

1994

• Marc Sadler

Marc Sadler Design
Asolo, Italy

EuroMusico
Centro Europeo per la Musica e il Teatro Musicale.

EuroMusico
Centro Europeo per la Musica e il Teatro Musicale.

ATTILIO ZAMPERONI

Casa G.F. Malipiero   Tel. 0330/007942
Foresto Vecchio, 7   fax.0423/55520
31031 Asolo (TV)

EuroMusico
Centro Europeo per la Musica e il Teatro Musicale.

Sede Provvisoria:
Casa G.F. Malipiero
Foresto Vecchio, 7
31031 Asolo (TV)

Tel.0330/667942
fax.0423/55526

**New identity after refurbishment
of a museum of urban transport**

1993

The identity combines stylized illustrations of travellers on London Transport in the last hundred years with the title of the museum set in Johnston's famous LTA alphabet, originally designed for London Transport and in itself one of the first classic corporate identities.

London Transport
Museum

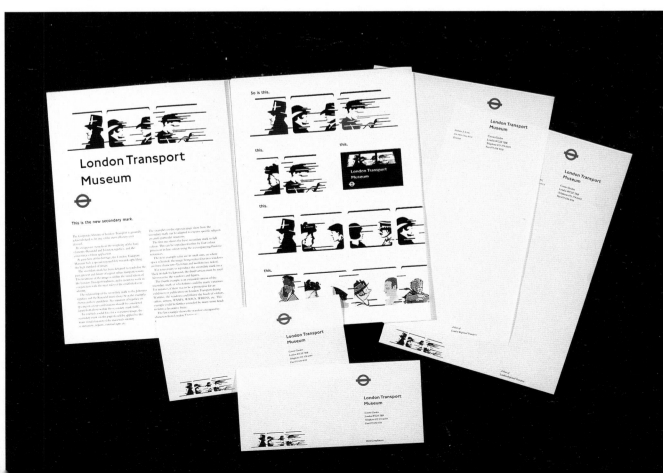

• **Crafts Council**
London, England

**Corporate identity and design
programme for a national body
promoting crafts and the crafts
professions**

1992

• John Rushworth, Vince Frost, Nick Finney

Pentagram Design Ltd.
London, England

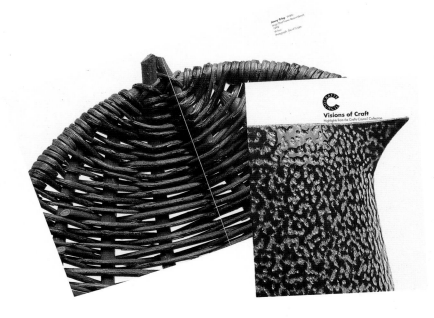

The Crafts Council needed a new identity both to mark a move to
new premises and to rekindle public awareness of the Council's
role as a promoter of crafts. The Council works through
exhibitions and displays, awards and publications, and an
information service, including an Index of Selected Makers which
lists some 500 craftspeople in Britain.

Pentagram's initial solution was a new logotype, based on a capital
letter C with the words Crafts and Council inscribed within the
letterform. To execute this Pentagram turned, appropriately
enough, to Tom Perkins, a letter cutter on the Index. After the
initial design was accepted, Pentagram were invited to consult on a
regular basis on the design of posters, catalogues and reports - on
all publications concerned with promoting the Council itself. Their
design for the 1992/3 Annual Report won a silver D&AD Award in
1994.

2010 – Textiles & New Technology at the Crafts Council Gallery 15 September to 13 November

colour into Cloth

A celebration of Britain's finest hand coloured textiles 1900 to 1994

14 April to 19 June
Crafts Council Gallery
44a Pentonville Road
Islington London N1 9BY
Telephone 071 278 7700

Free entry
Tuesday to Saturday 11-6
Sunday 2-6. Closed Monday
5 minutes from Angel tube

Organised in collaboration
with the Crafts Study Centre,
Holburne Museum Bath.

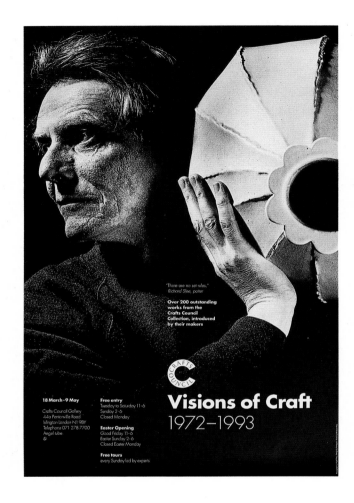

The Works exhibition catalogue and posters (above and facing).

English National Opera
London, England

Corporate image for national
opera company

1992

• Mike Dempsey

CDT Design Ltd.
London, England

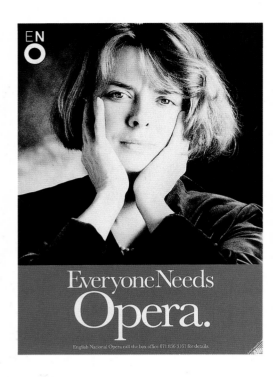

The English National Opera has an excellent reputation for its individual productions (always sung in English) but the management felt that their overall image needed to be reinforced. CDT's *fortissimo* solution was to use the three capital letters in increasing weights, and set the first two over a bold capital O. By going further in introducing a strict house style based on two typefaces only, the designers were also able to allow the individual productions to make their own statements, as in the posters shown here. This streamlining of the print output also created savings in budgets (allowing for more expenditure on photography, for example). The new identity, recognized by a Minerva award and a D&AD Silver, among others, has produced results in attracting both corporate sponsorship and new government grants.

Nothing against John,
Paul, George and Ringo.
But the Magical
Mystery Tour belongs
to Amadeus.

Arguably, W.A. Mozart is the world's most
successful travel agent.

For the last two hundred years, The
Magic flute has transported audience after
audience to a bewitchingly enchanted world.

"An opera that might have been
conceived by God" wrote one music critic.
(The Beatles' verdict is unrecorded).
We'd like you to judge for yourself at ENO's
production performed, as ever, in English.

A fairytale for all ages, you can sit
down to an evening of breathtaking sets,
achingly beautiful music and very witty
translation for between £5 and £48.
Full details are available on 071 632 8300.

Go on. Treat yourself with tickets
to a magical ride.

**Performances at the
London Coliseum from
October 20 to December 7**

EN
O

Where opera
comes alive

This evening
comes with
a safety warning.

A night at the opera isn't perhaps your idea
of living dangerously.

It is almost impossible, nevertheless,
to underestimate the sheer impact of a cast of
100, an orchestra of 100 and the remarkably
talented Willard White.

The opera in question is Musorgsky's
Khovanshchina. Chronicling Russia's two
most turbulent centuries, this is an ironclad
epic of unsurpassed resonance. Too much for
one man's lifetime, Stravinsky finished the
work and Shostakovich reorchestrated it.

You're invited to take your seats
at ENO. As usual this new production is in
English, and tickets are from £5 to £48.
Please call 071 632 8300 for details.

Like any ENO performance, there's
no standing on ceremony. Please just sit back
for your safety and comfort while we take
your soul for a ride.

**7 performances at the
London Coliseum from
November 24 to December 16**

EN
O

Where opera
comes alive

A series of four corporate advertisements, 1994.

**• Zeebelt Theater
The Hague, The Netherlands**

Evolving identity for a theatre

1992 onwards

• Gert Dunbar

Studio Dunbar
The Hague, The Netherlands

The Zeebelt Theater is not a theatre: it is considerably more than that. An independent arts centre, it has all the visual arts as well as dance and experimental theatre on its agenda. The association with Studio Dunbar, which creates posters, leaflets and print media, is a further expression of the forward thinking of the theatre, part of its comprehensive policy of communicating the contemporary. For Gert Dunbar, working with the Zeebelt is 'a new kind of corporate identity - an invisible one, if you like.' Certainly the work is the expression of a philosophy, rather than a rulebook, and its success has been marked by several design awards.

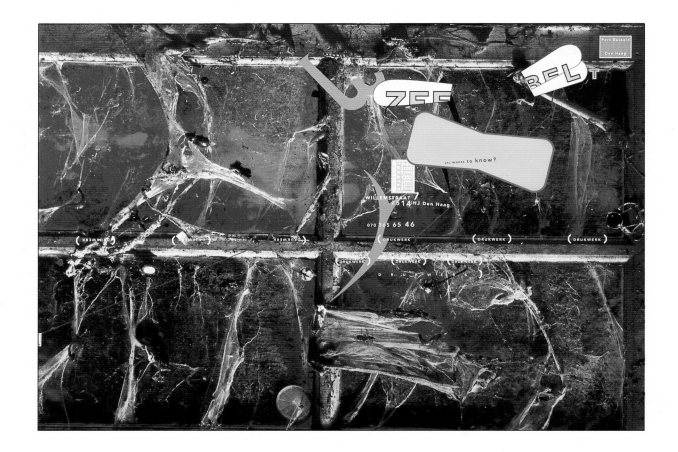

- **Sydney 2000**
  Sydney, Australia

  **Logo for Sydney's successful bid
  to host the Olympic Games in the
  year 2000**

  1993

- Minale Tattersfield & Partners
  Richmond, Surrey, England

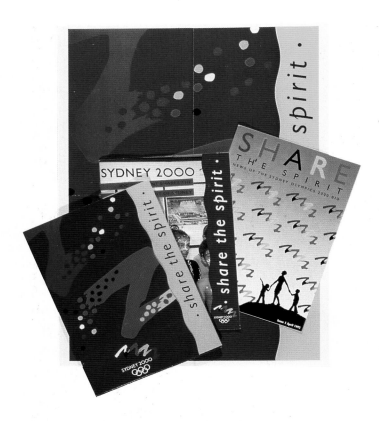

The logo for the Sydney Olympics needed to contain
the five linked Olympic rings and the five Olympic
colours, which are a consistent feature of all the
games. Minale Tattersfield's problem was to provide
an additional element that would express the vigour
and spirit of Sydney and Australia itself, and the
millennial event. The solution was to paint a line of
colour at the top, moving from sky to earth through
the colours of dawn - for the new century, moving
forward - for the Olympic flame's progress to the
Games, and moving through a series of pointed
arches - to echo the roofline of the Opera House,
Sydney's great landmark.

• **Nagano Winter Olympics
Nagano, Japan**

**Identity and mascot for the
Winter Olympic Games**

1992

• Landor Associates
San Francisco, USA, Tokyo, Japan

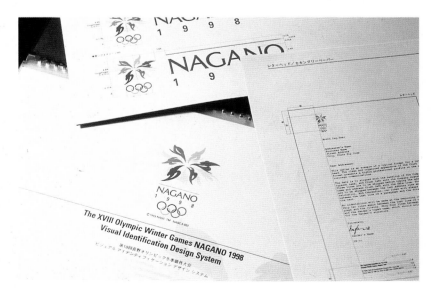

The identity for the Nagano Winter Olympics falls into two parts. There is the main logo, which adds a flower motif to the traditional Olympic rings. But a more popular image, unique to this event, was also needed, and this led to the Snowlets, a family of snowy owls intended as mascots to promote the games. To emphasize their informal character, the Snowlets are treated as if they were based on drawings by children.

SNOWLETS
スノーレッツ

- **The Public Theater**
New York, USA

**Identity, advertising, signage
for a theatre**

1994

- Paula Scher, Ron Louie, Liza Mazur

Pentagram Design
New York, USA

The Public Theater was famous both for its productions of new plays and for its annual Shakespeare Festival in Central Park in Manhattan, under the direction of the late Joseph Papp. The new director, George C. Wolfe, turned to Pentagram to design an identity that would re-establish the theatre's accessibility and broad appeal. Pentagram devised a streetwise programme, based on a bold and active sans serif lettering. This textual choice both echoes the vibrant tradition of theatre posters (wood faces were used as models for the lettering) and works within the brash visual language of graffito and street display in New York. The programme was applied to signs, T-shirts, advertising and banners within and outside the theatre building.

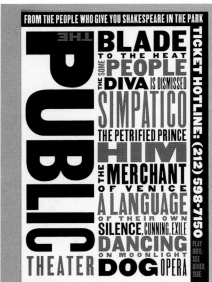

• **The Fashion Center**
New York, USA

Logo and signage for a fashion
design organization

1993

• Michael Bierut, Paula Scher, Esther Bridavsky

Pentagram Design
New York, USA

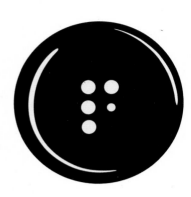

THE
FASHION
CENTER

The Fashion Center comprises over 170,000 designers, manufacturers, stylists, models, wholesalers and fashion retailers in mid-town Manhattan. The Center is organized as a 'business improvement district' and was formed by property owners who wanted to take an active role in improving their urban environment. Among their concerns are subjects such as private security, sanitation and services, as well as marketing and promotional programmes for the members.

• **IDI**
London, England

**Corporate identity and posters for
an annual interior design show**

1992

• David Hillman, Lucy Holmes

Pentagram Design Ltd.
London, England

Interior Design International hosts an
annual show of interiors in London. The
main logotype comprises the initial letters
of the organization but with an orange
circle for the bowl of the capital D. On
the posters a range of interior objects,
ranging from a bath plug to a Tiffany lamp
have been substituted for the circle.

Design companies

In the following accounts of design companies these abbreviations have been used

AGI - Alliance Graphique Internationale, Switzerland

AIA - American Institute of Architecture

AIGA - American Institute of Graphic Arts

BNO - Boertsvereining Nederlandse Ontwerpers (Dutch Association for Design)

D&AD - Design and Art Direction, awards and publications, London

ICOGRADA - International Council of Graphic Design Associations

JAGDA - Japan Graphic Designers Association

MoMA - Museum of Modern Art, New York

V&A - Victoria & Albert Museum, London

The work in this book was selected by Wally Olins between October and December 1994, after a worldwide free and open call for entries.

The editors wish to thank the BNO, the American Center for Design, the Chartered Society of Designers and the AGI for their assistance in the call for entries, as well as Peter Lux, Horst Liebermann, Joanne Lightfoot and Jon Turner for their help and advice with the preparation of this book.

BBV

Zurich, Switzerland

Founded in Zurich in 1968, BBV now has offices in Lyon and Milan, and specializes in corporate communications and design for a range of national and international clients.

Professor Michael Baviera trained at the Kunstgewerbe-schule, Zurich. The author of various books and articles on design, he has been professor at the institute for communications design at the Fachhochschule at Konstanz in Germany since 1987.

Blaich Associates

Aspen, Colorado, USA

Dr. Robert Blaich founded this consultancy in Aspen four years ago, providing management consultancy to a range of international companies including Philips and Texas Instruments.

Robert Blaich trained as an architect, and then joined the American furniture company Herman Miller, where he became vice president of design and development. He then became managing director of Corporate Industrial Design for Philips in 1980, retiring in 1992 to work with his own design consultancy.

Studio Boot

's-Hertogenbosch, The Netherlands

Studio Boot was set up in 1992. Their strongly visual work can be found on film and theatre posters and on exhibition catalogues and invitations. In May 1995 the Dutch postal service, the PTT, issued a stamp designed by Studio Boot, who had also designed the cover for the 1992 PTT annual report. Their work has been exhibited in New York, Mexico City and Cologne. In 1944 they designed the member's yearbook of the BNO, the Dutch graphic artists' association.

Petra Janssen worked with Nucleus Design in London and at Studio Dunbar before becoming one of the two founding partners of Studio Boot.

Edwin Vollebergh studied with Petra Janssen at the Royal School of Art in 's-Hertogenbosch, and worked for Studio Alkmaar for two years before co-founding Studio Boot.

Carter Wong & Partners

London, England

In 1994 Carter Wong & Partners celebrated their tenth anniversary. The partnership was started by Philip Carter and Philip Wong, and has since expanded to become part of CWSH Designers, offering three-dimensional design services as well as graphics. Their client list includes the Fédération Internationale de l'Automobile, Cable & Wireless plc and ICI Paints.

Philip Wong was senior designer at Brewer Jones before founding Carter Wong & Partners. A member of D&AD and the Design Business Association, Philip Wong has been a juror for the D&AD awards, an advisor to the Council on National Academic Awards and external assessor for Liverpool Polytechnic graphic design degrees.

CDT Design Ltd.

London, England

CDT, formerly Carroll, Dempsey and Thirkell, named after the founding partners, was founded in 1979. The graphic design consultancy handles a wide range of clients, particularly in the film, leisure and cultural field. They are frequent prizewinners in national and international design competitions: the graphic identity for the English National Opera has probably won more awards than any other in the last decade.

Ian Chilvers worked for Pentagram, particularly on the implementation of a new identity for the publishers Faber & Faber, before joining CDT eight years ago. His current client list includes UBS Phillips and Drew, The Willis Group and The British Land Company plc.

Mike Dempsey has spent the last thirty years working as a graphic designer, first in publishing and then at the agency he founded. He has won eight gold and silver D&AD awards, among other awards, and in November 1994 he received the prestigious appointment of Royal Designer to Industry, placing him among the top 100 designers in Britain.

Alan Chan Design Co

Wanchai, Hong Kong

Alan Chan started his independent design practice in Hong Kong eight years ago. He specializes in retail and corporate design.

CIAC

Barcelona, Spain

CIAC (Centro de Investigatión y Aplicaciones de la Communicación) was founded in 1975 by Joan Costa, the current company president. The company is involved, through different professional disciplines, with all aspects of business communications strategy. A Spanish company with an international structure, CIAC has offices in Barcelona, Madrid, Lisbon, Mexico City, Paris and Brussels. They have public and private sector clients in their portfolio, including the Banco Nacional Ultramarino in Portugal and the Mexico City Airport.

Albert Culleré, creative director and design director, represented Spain at the 1988 Oslo conference for the International Year of Graphic Design. He is also professor of visual identity at the ICE in Barcelona, design director of the *Enciclopedia di Diseño*, and a member of the Spanish design associations BEDA and AIGA.

Daniel Panicello, director of visual communications, is the co-founder of the Graphic Research Laboratory, Barcelona. His work has been widely exhibited in Europe and in South America.

Coley Porter Bell

London, England

Founded in 1979, Coley Porter Bell has grown from a small design studio into a leading corporate and brand identity consultants, with a European and international client base, and billings of £5 million annually. The practice employs a staff of over 65 business consultants, marketing specialists, and graphic and products designers.

Simon Carter, senior designer, literature, worked on many computer, business and lifestyle magazines, and as a freelance corporate identity and literature designer before joining Coley Porter Bell in 1994.

Stephen Franks, creative director, corporate, joined Coley Porter Bell in 1983. He graduated from the London College of Printing in 1979, and has seventeen years experience of corporate identity design. He is a member of D&AD, and a Fellow of the Royal Society of Arts.

Judith Johnston, designer, joined Coley Porter Bell in 1989 after graduating with a BA from Duncan of Jordanstone College of Art, Dundee.

Alexander Demuth Agentur

Frankfurt am Main, Germany

Alexander Demuth founded his agency in 1985, specializing in an integrated communication service covering advertising, public relations, corporate design and communications consultancy. The company now has twenty-five full-time staff and fifteen part-time associates. With partner companies in New York, Detroit and Vienna, Demuth's client list includes major German and international corporations such as Hyundai, ITT, DG Bank, Quelle, NTV and Sal. Oppenheim Junior & Co.

Alexander Demuth, chairman, worked in journalism, advertising and PR in Germany and New York before starting the agency. He is the author of various books and specialist publications on corporate design.

Peter Kraus graduated in communications design and worked at major agencies such as Ogilvy & Mather and Saatchi & Saatchi before joining Alexander Demuth where he is creative director.

Birgit Stähling was art director for the Bank of Scotland, and worked at Saatchi & Saatchi. She is now art director at Alexander Demuth.

Diefenbach Elkins

San Francisco and New York, USA

Founded in 1990, Diefenbach Elkins offers an integrated consulting service to large service companies. In this their Megatrends research service is particularly important. Their client list includes a number of major airlines and travel companies, petrochemical companies, financial service companies and manufacturers. The group has branch offices in South America, Spain, Belgium, Germany, Hungary and Malaysia.

John Diefenbach was chief executive officer of Landor Associates until Landor was sold to Young and Rubicam in 1989. His clients at Diefenbach Elkins range from Kodak, Master Card and Motorola to Saudia Airlines, US West and KPMG Peat Marwick. He is a frequent lecturer at university and business management seminars in the USA and Europe.

Robert Kahn, senior vice-president and marketing strategy director, studied at the University of Pennsylvania and was granted a top MBA from Pepperdine University. His particular speciality is with clients in the airline industry.

Angelika Preston, born in Germany and educated in Canada, is a founding principal of Diefenbach Elkins and currently vice-president and design director. Her client list concentrates on companies in the service and leisure industries.

Claude Salzberger, executive vice-president and creative director, has over fifteen years experience of corporate and brand identity consultancy for international firms. He was previously at Landor Associates in San Francisco. His experience of airline work includes Air Canada, Alcazar, Iberia and Aeromexico.

Din Graphics

London, England

Din Graphics was founded in 1989, and has rapidly achieved a major role in the graphic design field, particularly for retailing and fashion. Clients have included French Connection, Ralph Lauren, the George Davies Partnership, W.H. Smith, ATT and Mothercare (UK) Ltd. Work in the cultural field has included projects for the V&A Museum and the Arts Council.

Valerie Wickes, founder and managing partner of Din Graphics, trained at St Martins School of Art in London. She was art director at Laura Ashley before starting Din, as well as working extensively with Next on the first Next Directory and with further Next brands.

Studio Dunbar

The Hague, The Netherlands

Studio Dunbar was founded in 1977. Their client list is a roll-call of some of the most design-conscious companies in the Netherlands and in Europe, including the Dutch PTT, the Rijksmuseum, the Dutch Railways, Philips, Apple Computers Europe, IBM and Zanders Papiere. They have seven silver and two gold D&AD awards to their credit, and eight awards from the Dutch Art Directors Club.

Gert Dunbar was a postgraduate student at the Royal College of Art in London, and returned to head the graphics department there as visiting professor from 1985-87. After founding a graphic design division for Tel Design, he set up Studio Dunbar. A member of AGI, he is a past chairman on the BNO and past president of the British D&AD.

Halpin Grey Vermeir

London, England

Founded in 1987, Halpin Grey Vermeir specialize in corporate communications. Their client list includes British Rail, the National Union of Teachers, Royal Mail Stamps, Unilever and Mobil. Their work has frequently appeared in D&AD annuals, and in 1991 and 1992 they won the *Design Week* annual Best Corporate Identity Award, and in 1993 a Euro Best Award.

Kenya Hara

Tokyo, Japan

Born in 1958 in Okayama Prefecture, Kenya Hara joined the Nippon Design Center in 1989. He has been art director of the Takeo Paper World exhibition since 1989. He has received two Mainoni Advertising Design Awards, a Kodak Photo Calendar Prize, a JAGDA New Talent Award and Tokyo Art Directors Club Prizes in 1990 and 1991.

HM+E Incorporated

Toronto, Canada

HM+E Incorporated is a Canadian-owned design and marketing firm, founded in 1991 by Paul Haslip and Karen Eensild. Annual reports and corporate brochures as well as identities, print advertising and sales promotional materials figure largely in their workload. Clients include Ontario Blue Cross, BT Bank of Canada, and the World Wildlife Fund. The firm has particular strength in the real estate field, with clients such as Daniels Development, Canada Homes, and the Venturon Corporation.

Paul Haslip was a Design Canada scholar at St Martins School of Art in London, and past president of the Ontario chapter of the Society of Graphic Designers of Canada. A founder of HM+E, his work has been recognized in awards from the AIGA, and the Art Directors Clubs of Toronto, New York and Los Angeles.

Hornall Anderson Design Works

Seattle, USA

Jack Hornall and *Jack Anderson* founded their design partnership in 1982, and it is now one of the largest and most respected design firms on the West Coast of America. As well as corporate design, the practice works on environmental graphics and signage, packaging and promotional graphics. A team-based approach is used, closely related to each client's marketing needs. Their client base includes all sizes of companies, from those in the *Fortune 500* to new business start-ups.

Intégral Concept / Ruedi Baur et Associés

Montreuil-Paris, France

Ruedi Baur et Associés was set up in Paris in 1989. They provide graphic design and identity services to cultural, social and administrative bodies, including the Centre Georges Pompidou, the Fondation Cartier, the Musée Picasso and the Cité des Sciences et de l'Industrie.

Ruedi Baur was born in Paris in 1956. After studying in Zurich, he formed BBV with Michael Baviera and Peter Vetter. In 1988 he returned to Paris and set up Intégral Concept with Pippo Lionni. He is a member of the AGI, and his work has been exhibited in France and Germany. Since 1990 he has been working with the Ecole des Beaux-Arts in Lyon on the development of a postgraduate programme in two- and three-dimensional design.

I & G - Investigación Gráfica
Madrid, Spain

Founded in 1975, I&G rapidly became a leading company in the development of corporate identities for the public sector in Spain, with clients such as the Ministerio de Obras Publicas y Urbanismo, the Junta de Andalucía and the Comunidad de la Rioja. Since then the company has moved into the additional fields of product design, urban furniture and editorial design. Their client list for corporate identity now includes some of Spain's largest industrial concerns, banks and public services, including the national railways, and their work has won numerous awards.

Alberto Corazón, born in 1942, worked as a freelance designer before starting his own publishing company in 1973. Alberto Corazón Editor published some of the first books in Spanish on semiotics and product design. Since founding I&G he has also written several books on design, and is well-known as a design journalist.

K₂ Design
Tokyo, Japan

The K₂ office was set up in 1969 by Keisuke Nagatomo and Seitaro Kuroda. In 1982 an exhibition of the partnership's work, the K₂ Cultural Monuments Exhibition, was held in Tokyo and Osaka.

Keisuke Nagatomo was born in Osaka in 1939. As well as art directing editorials, advertisements and events he has worked extensively as a book illustrator and writer. His poster work is in the collection of MoMA, New York, and he has been honoured by the Japan Advertising Artists Club.

Kojitani, Irie & Inc.
Tokyo, Japan

Kojitani, Irie & Inc. was founded in 1972, to work with clients in retail and graphic design. In 1986 the agency received the gold design prize awarded by the Japanese ministry of international trade and industry.

Hiroshi Kojitani was born in Nara in 1937 and worked in Tokyo and Paris before forming Kojitani, Irie & Inc. He is an expert on wine, with the titles of *Chevalier de Champagne* and *Sommelier d'Honneur.*

Kensuke Irie was born in 1941 in Kagoshima, and worked at Nippon Rayon and Ginza Matsuya before setting up Kojitani, Irie & Inc. Also an oenophile, he holds the title of *Kikisake-shi,* or rice wine *sommelier.*

Landor Associates
San Francisco, USA, and worldwide

Landor, with well over three hundred staff around the globe, is the largest identity consultancy and design company in the world. The company was founded by Walter Landor over fifty years ago, and at the end of the 1950s pioneered consumer pre-testing and research techniques through their Consumer Research Centre and their Image Power reports, now an industry standard for quantifying brand strength. Landor's philosophy that a company is as much a brand as is a packaged product has benefited a large list of international clients such as Daimler-Benz, Alitalia, L'Oreal, Coca-Cola, British Airways and Montedison.

Richard Ford, executive creative director, Landor Associates London, trained as an architect, and worked as an architect and interior designer on many public, hotel and office projects. He joined Landor Associates eleven years ago, and his client list includes Royal Mail, Alfred Dunhill, Chase Manhattan Europe and Deutsche Shell.

Andrew Glidden is an associate design director responsible for creative direction and project management in the branded environments group. With Landor Associates since 1987, he has been working in the Hong Kong office since January 1994, to launch the Cathay Pacific identity.

Lewis Moberly
London, England

Lewis Moberly is internationally known for packaging, graphic and corporate identity design. Set up in 1984, the company employs thirty-five people, including designers, project managers and support staff. Their list of awards includes three gold and silver D&AD awards, and a *Design-Week* prize for packaging design.

McIlroy Coates
Edinburgh, Scotland

This design company, founded in 1981 and based in Leith, the seaport of Edinburgh, has wide experience of corporate identity design and implementation in both the public and private sector. Interior design is also a speciality. Their team of fifteen designers, with supporting product and business development staff, are led by four design directors. Their work has won design awards internationally and nationally: a McIlroy Coates project was the overall winner of the first Scottish Design Awards in 1994.

Andrew Hunter, managing director, trained in graphics at Edinburgh School of Art. He joined McIlroy Coates in 1987, after eight years as joint managing director of the Tayburn Design Group. A member of D&AD and a fellow of the Chartered Society of Designers, he is the 1994 chairman of the Design Business Association in Scotland.

Graham Scott, design director, trained at the Glasgow School of Art and St Martins School of Art, London, graduating in 1985. He joined McIlroy Coates in 1987, becoming design director in 1992.

Mendell & Oberer
Munich, Germany

Mendell & Oberer is one of the most respected design firms in Southern Germany, with a long list of national and international design awards and a strong clientele of German and European companies.

Millford - Van Den Berg Design
Wassenaar, The Netherlands

Millford-van den Berg is a specialized design company. They create and develop product packaging and corporate design programmes. From the outset their objective has been to approach design as a strategic business tool. Their staff includes twenty-five design experts in different fields including desk-top publishing and visualization, together with project managers. Two guiding principles for the agency are immediate and direct contact between designer and client, and full financial transparency. Their client list includes Akzo Nobel, Christie's, Holland Casinos and the Scheepvaart Museum.

Dennis de Rond, art director for corporate design, moved into design after studying art. He joined Millford-van den Berg in 1993, and is 28 years old.

Jos van der Zwaal worked for a number of design companies including Ten Cate Bergmans before joining Millford-van den Berg in 1987. He is now creative director for corporate design.

Minale Tattersfield & Partners
Richmond, Surrey, England

Minale Tattersfield's famous 'scribble' logo highlights what has been called the keynote of the firm, that style should only be the servant of the design solution. Founded by Brian Tattersfield and Marcello Minale in 1964, and now with a further four main partners in the UK, the company is well-known for its corporate design and brand development work, with a clutch of national and international awards to its credit. Marcello Minale grew up in postwar Naples, and later worked with the Finnish designer Tapio Wirkkala. Brian Tattersfield studied at the Royal College of Art in the early 1960s, and numbers Charles Eames and Saul Bass among his key influences. The combination of their two very diverse talents has provided the driving force of Minale Tattersfield for thirty years, as the company has grown to include Design Strategy, a parallel agency in Paris, and branch offices in twelve other countries world-wide. And as a matter of policy all work is credited to the firm, rather than to individual designers.

Arcadi Moradell & Associados
Barcelona, Spain

Arcadi Moradell founded his first design studio in 1969, forming Moradell & Associados in the early 1980s. In the last twenty-five years he has created over 500 corporate identities, brands and logos, for public bodies, national and international companies, and professional associations. He played a major design role in the Barcelona Olympics of 1992. He is also involved in the promotion of design in Spain through awards and education, a role recognized by his appointment in 1993 as Vice-President of ICOGRADA.

Kenzo Nakagawa
Tokyo, Japan

Kenzo Nagakawa was born in Osaka in 1947. After working in retail advertising and design, he set up Bolt and Nuts Studio, with Kumiko Nagasaki and Hiroyasu Nobuyama. In 1975 he joined the Nippon Design Center, where he is now art director. His clientele includes the Isetan Department Store. His work has won a Tokyo Art Directors Club prize in 1979, and the special prize at the Brno Biennale in 1980, among other awards.

9-D Design
Zurich, Switzerland

This co-operative partnership of graphic designers offers a range of client services including print design, corporate identity, packaging and advertising.

Richard Feurer and *Christian Hugin* trained in Zurich before joining forces in 9-D Design.

One Ahead Graphic Design Studio
St Ives, NSW, Australia

Raphael Klaesi studied graphic design and typography both in Britain and his native Switzerland before emigrating to Australia some twenty years ago. There he has worked in larger agencies and in teaching design at university level. He preferred, however, to set up his own small agency with a list of selected clients, mainly from the world of the media.

The Partners
London, England

In 1991 *Design Week* magazine published their first annual survey of the hundred most creative design companies: The Partners came first, as they have in every annual survey since. There are seven partners in all, five design partners, a strategy and a financial partner, with a total staff of forty-three. Specialists in corporate identity, their clientele includes a large range of financial, professional, retail, industrial and public clients. In 1993, this included nine of the fifty largest companies in Europe, according to the *Financial Times 500*.

James Beveridge joined The Partners in 1984, and became a Design Partner four years later. His clients include Cellnet, Commercial Union, Leica, and Mencap. His work has regularly been included in design annuals and exhibitions.

Steve Gibbons obtained his Masters degree from the Royal College of Art. His list of awards includes two D&AD Silvers, Letterhead Awards, and in the USA, awards from the Art Directors Club of New York. His clients include British Airways, Harrods, Unilever and Woolworths.

Pentagram Design
London and New York

Fletcher/Forbes/Gill was one of the leading design agencies in London in the 1960s, and the progenitor of Pentagram, launched in 1972. Since then Pentagram has grown to a main partnership of sixteen, with one hundred and ten support staff, and offices in New York, San Francisco, Austin and Hong Kong. But the original spirit of creative independence for the partners with shared support has been maintained, particularly through Colin Forbes' role as chair of the partners' meetings. Pentagram's consistent philosophy of design, enriched by new opportunities and the involvement of new partners, is one of its fundamental strengths, leading to a gallery of creative work on individual projects and an unmatched reputation for quality design. The design activities of Pentagram range from identity, branding and packaging projects to exhibition design, interior designs, architectural services and product design.

James Biber trained at Cornell University's College of Architecture and was head of his own practice in New York before joining Pentagram New York as a partner in 1991. He now heads Pentagram Architectural Services. His work has won awards from the New York Chapter of the AIA, the Industrial Designers Society of America and the Architectural League.

Michael Bierut, born in 1958, was vice-president of graphic design at Vignelli Associates before joining Pentagram New York as a partner in 1990. His work is in the permanent collection of MoMA, New York, the Metropolitan Museum of Art, New York, and the Musée des Arts Décoratifs, Montreal. He was elected a member of AGI in 1989.

Peter Harrison studied at the London School of Printing before emigrating to the USA, where he ran his own design office in New York. He joined Pentagram as a partner in 1979. His current portfolio includes projects on corporate promotion, annual reports and sales material.

David Hillman, born in Oxford in 1943, worked in newspaper design before becoming art director and then deputy editor of *Nova* in 1968. He joined Pentagram as a partner in 1978, continuing to work on editorial design. In 1989 his redesign of *The Guardian* newspaper won a D&AD silver award, one of the four he has won to date.

Woody Pirtle was born in Texas in 1944. After running his own agency in Dallas for a decade he moved to New York in 1988, becoming a partner in Pentagram. Clients include the Rockefeller Foundation, U&lc magazine, Rizzoli Publishing and the 1994 World Cup Organizing Committee.

John Rushworth graduated in 1981, joining Pentagram two years later. In 1990, he was invited to become a partner, being the first partner to be appointed from within the

company. His design for the 1991-2 Crafts Council annual report won a silver D&AD award.

Paula Scher formed her own firm with Terry Koppel in 1984, joining Pentagram New York as a partner in 1991. She has received more than 300 awards from international design associations. She is chairman of the graduate programme in graphic design at the School of Visual Arts, where she has taught a senior course for the last nine years.

Roundel Design Group
London, England

Founded as an independent in 1982, Roundel Design Group have been consistently placed in the top five of Britain's 'hot 100' design companies over the last five years, according to *Design* magazine's annual surveys. Their work in corporate identity, promotional literature, packaging and advertising has won many awards worldwide. Clients include companies in financial and professional services, media, education, manufacturing, retail, automotive, distribution, railway and postal services. Their corporate identity projects are used as design management study examples by London Business School MBA students.

Michael Denny is the managing and design director of Roundel Design Group. His portfolio includes many leading companies such as Bovis, Railfreight and the Royal Mail, for whom he recently designed the £10 postage stamp.

John Bateson joined Roundel Design Group in 1979. He is now joint partner and design director. His previous work included being senior designer at the Open University, and he still plays an active role in design education.

Harold Batten, who is 44, trained at the London College of Printing and is now senior designer and a director of Roundel Design Group. His recent projects include signage for the Docklands Light Railway.

Deborah Osborne, senior designer at Roundel Design Group, has been with the company for the last four years. Her recent projects include the livery for the Class 92 Channel Tunnel locomotive.

Michéle Bury worked in Paris on the identity for the Château de Versailles before joining Roundel Design Group one year ago.

Jeremy Roots worked for the publishing company Reed International before joining Roundel Design Group one year ago.

Marc Sadler Design
Asolo, Italy

Marc Sadler graduated in industrial design at the Ecole Nationale Supérieure des Arts Décoratifs in Paris. As an industrial designer he has specialized in working with high-technology plastics and glasses. His work in products for outdoor sports, particularly ski boots, and now lighting and furniture, has been widely recognized. Corporate identity is a new aspect of his design business, which has a New York studio as well as the main office in the Veneto.

Siegel & Gale
New York & London

Siegel & Gale was founded in 1969 and is now a worldwide organization specializing in all aspects of corporate and marketing communications. The company has four operating groups, Corporate and Brand Identity, Simplified Communications, Interactive Media and Corporate Advertising, and an international client base of over 200 major corporations, financial institutions and associations. They are strongly involved in the creation of simplified legal and business documentation, an area they pioneered over ten years ago, and, more recently, have developed multimedia electronic communications systems for managing corporate identity and marketing design programmes.

Sondra Adams, associate design director, is an honours graduate of Philadelphia College of Art, and her recent projects include a literature system for IDS/American Express and corporate identity for The Wyatt Company.

Kenneth R. Cooke is creative director, responsible for design and creative strategy on corporate and brand identity assignments worldwide. Before joining the agency he worked for Frankfurt Gips Balkind, Landor Associates and IDENTICA, of which he was a founder and partner. His work has been widely published, and recognized in awards by the AIGA, the Society of Typographic Arts, the New York Art Directors Club and other bodies.

Raul Gutierrez, design director, has degrees in communications and graphic design from the University of Santo Thomas in the Philippines and the Pratt Institute, New York. Prior to joining Siegel & Gale he worked for Landor Associates and Modi & Beckler Design. His current responsibilities include design development, naming, strategic planning and implementation.

The Team
London, England

Founded in 1989, The Team specialize in corporate identity, packaging and branding. Their client list ranges from small professional groups to major retailers in the UK and Europe.

Tel Design
The Hague, The Netherlands

Tel Design was founded in 1962 as an industrial design group. With the creation of a graphic design wing, at first under Gert Dunbar, the company rapidly developed into one of the leading corporate identity specialists in the Netherlands. Tel Design works with a wide range of clients in commerce and industry, as well as with long-standing public sector clients, especially in healthcare, education and energy (such as Gasunie and NUON in the energy sector). With a staff of sixteen, Tel Design also undertakes exhibition design and signage projects.

Gert Kootstra, born 1962, became deputy director in 1994. He trained at the Constantijn Hugens Academy in Kampen, and worked at the SDU (Dutch state publishing house) before joining Tel Design in 1990.

Ronald van Lit, born 1958, was educated at the Sint Joost Academy in Breda and joined Tel Design in 1987. He was appointed team leader in 1992.

Paul Vermijs was born in 1950. After studying at the Sint Joost Academy in Breda he joined Tel Design in 1980, becoming team leader in 1982 and a director in 1988.

Visser Bay Anders Toscani
Amsterdam, The Netherlands

Visser Bay Anders Toscani Design was formed in 1984, the first company in Holland to offer both corporate identity and brand development services for an increasingly design-aware market. The company has thirty-six employees, a mix of designers and marketeers led by a management of two creative directors and a financial director.

Eugene Bay studied at the London College of Printing and worked in London before moving to Holland in 1981. He is the founder and creative director of Visser Bay Anders Toscani Design, and since 1990 has been chairman of the BNO.

Teun Anders, joint founder and creative director of Visser Bay Anders Toscani Design, studied at the Rotterdam Academie. He worked at Young & Rubicam, where he founded The Design House, the design wing of Young & Rubicam. Since 1991 he has been a board member of the BNO.

Pieta Booy, financial director, studied management and finance,. She then worked in advertising with Hansnel and DMM/Result, where she was deputy managing director before moving to Visser Bay Anders Toscani Design in 1990.

de Vringer
The Hague, The Netherlands

A small design partnership specializing in corporate identity, packaging, print graphics and advertising, de Vringer was formed in 1991. Their work for CBK Dordrecht has been awarded a BNO prize.

The Workroom
London, England

Formed in 1990 by Martin Devlin and Brigid McMullen, The Workroom specializes in design for print and corporate identity. Clients include CIMA and Coates Viyella, as well as a strong list of charities, including the National Asthma Campaign, Action on Smoking and Health, Quit, and the British Epilepsy Association. Their annual report for the epilepsy association won a design prize in 1994, and their work has been published in the D&AD annuals for 1991, 1993 and 1994.

Martin Devlin worked at Minale Tattersfield & Partners, before working at The Partners as a senior designer. He then spent two years setting up a corporate design unit at Dewe Rogerson with Brigid McMullen before starting The Workroom, where he is partner and joint creative principal.

Brigid McMullen, partner and joint creative principal, worked at Fitch & Company before joining The Partners for three years, and then moving to Dewe Rogerson.

XMPR
London, England

XMPR was started as a management buy-out of Michael Peters Retail in 1990. Corporate identity is one of the main areas the core staff of eighteen now cover, the other being retail and commercial interior design. Current and recent clients include the Argyll Group, BAA (their Club Europe lounge at Heathrow Airport won a *Design Week* award), Bank of Ireland, Ellesse, Gruppo Rinascente, Harrods, Lego, Mercury Communications and Yapi Credi.

Rob Davie, who qualified in three-dimensional design at Kingston University in England, is the managing director of XMPR, having joined the Michael Peters Group in 1981 and later leading the management buy-out. As he was born in Italy and is fluent in Italian, he has brought considerable understanding to the firm's dealings with major Italian clients.

Vassoula Vasiliou has an MA in graphic design from the Royal College of Art in London. Formerly associate design director at Fitch RS, she is now creative director at XMPR.

Zintzmeyer & Lux
Zurich, Switzerland

Founded by Peter Lux and Jörg Zintzmeyer over twenty years ago, Zintzmeyer & Lux has evolved from a small agency into an internationally active company providing a wide range of consultancy services. These range from the development of corporate design through specific behavioural and structural solutions to communication problems and brand identity consulting.

Index of designers, *clients*, and **design companies**.